UDIES IN ENGLISH LITERATURE No. 4

General Editor

D1352844

eady published in the series:

Already published in the series (*continued*):

THE POETRY OF
W. B. YEATS

by

A. NORMAN JEFFARES

Professor of English
University of Stirling

EDWARD ARNOLD

First published 1961 by
Edward Arnold (Publishers) Ltd.
41 Bedford Square, London WC1B 3DQ

Reprinted 1963, 1964, 1967, 1970, 1973
Reprinted with amended bibliography 1976
Reprinted 1979

ISBN 0 7131 5059 9

To David Webb

Printed and bound in Great Britain at
The Camelot Press Ltd, Southampton

General Preface

The object of this series is to provide studies of individual novels, plays and groups of poems and essays which are known to be widely read by students. The emphasis is on clarification and evaluation; biographical and historical facts, while they may be discussed when they throw light on particular elements in a writer's work, are generally subordinated to critical discussion. What kind of work is this? What exactly goes on here? How good is this work, and why? These are the questions that each writer will try to answer.

It should be emphasized that these studies are written on the assumption that the reader has already read carefully the work discussed. The objective is not to enable students to deliver opinions about works they have not read, nor is it to provide ready-made ideas to be applied to works that have been read. In one sense all critical interpretation can be regarded as foisting opinions on readers, but to accept this is to deny the advantages of any sort of critical discussion directed at students or indeed at anybody else. The aim of these studies is to provide what Coleridge called in another context 'aids to reflection' about the works discussed. The interpretations are offered as suggestive rather than as definitive, in the hope of stimulating the reader into developing further his own insights. This is after all the function of all critical discourse among sensible people.

Because of the interest which this kind of study has aroused, it has been decided to extend it first from merely English literature to include also some selected works of American literature and now further to include selected works in English by Commonwealth writers. The criterion will remain that the book studied is important in itself and is widely read by students.

DAVID DAICHES

Acknowledgements

The author and publishers wish to express their thanks to Mrs. W. B. Yeats, to Macmillan & Company Ltd., publishers of the *Collected Poems*, and to the Macmillan Company of New York for their kind permission to reproduce quotations from the work of W. B. Yeats.

Contents

1. *The Wanderings of Oisin*

The first period of Yeats's poetry extends from early writings published in the *Dublin University Review* from 1883 to the poems included in *The Wind Among the Reeds* of 1899. Within these fifteen years he progressed from local poetry to national, from national to European. His first poems reflect a gentle dreaminess, a preoccupation with solitary figures—heroes, sages, poets, magicians; while melancholia enwraps the weakly limpid descriptions of scenery in *The Island of Statues*, an arcadian play full of Spenserian and Shelleyan touches. Dreaming, perhaps poetry itself, was a defence against the world for Yeats, who at eighteen 'lived breathed ate drank and slept poetry', and was sensitive and shy.

His father, J. B. Yeats the artist, influenced him greatly, read aloud his own favourite poems to him, encouraged him to write, taught him that a gentleman was not concerned with 'getting on' in life, and sent him to the School of Art in Dublin so that he could resolve his doubts as to whether his career should be that of artist or writer. His family friends were certain he was to be famous, and his father encouraged the idea most of all. But though J. B. Yeats, a forceful sceptic, was an impressive debater and talker, his son wanted to believe, and hurled himself headlong into the pursuit of truth. For Yeats this meant trying to find a substitute for religion, searching for a language of symbols, as he tells us in *Autobiographies*:

> I am very religious, and deprived by Huxley and Tyndall, whom I detested, of the simple minded religion of my childhood. I had made a new religion, almost an infallible Church of poetic tradition, of a fardel of stories, and of personages, and of emotions, inseparable from their first expression, passed on from generation to generation by poets and painters with some help from philosophers and theologians.[1]

His search led him into forming a Hermetic Society in 1885 and there professing that the philosophy in poetry was the only permanent

[1] W. B. Yeats, *Autobiographies*, 1956, p. 115.

authoritative religion. In his adolescent loneliness he combined pre-Raphaelite weariness and a languorous delicacy of perception. All action and words leading to it seemed to him even more vulgar or trivial after a Brahmin, Mohini Chatterjee, had come to lecture about Theosophy in Dublin (an influence recorded in 'The Indian upon God'[1] and looked back upon in 'Mohini Chatterjee').[2] Instead he developed a plaintive belief that 'words alone are certain good' in 'The Song of the Happy Shepherd'[3] and a dreaming of escape from life in 'The Sad Shepherd'.[4]

Yet at the same time, under the influence of John O'Leary, a former Fenian leader, Yeats developed an interest in Irish nationalism, read Irish patriotic literature and joined a Young Ireland society. He realised he must make himself a style and have 'things to write about that the ballad writers might be the better'. He formed an ambition to write a new kind of Irish literature, and came nearer to creating a style of his own when he began to write about what he knew: the scenery of Sligo where he lived as a child (for which he had longed when at school in the later 1870's in England) and the folklore to which his imagination responded when as a young man he spent later summers in Sligo with his uncle George Pollexfen. From Sligo and its stories of ghosts and fairies came characteristic cadences in 'The Stolen Child':

> Where the wave of moonlight glosses
> The dim grey sands with light,
> Far off by furthest Rosses
> We foot it all the night,
> Weaving olden dances,
> Mingling hands and mingling glances
> Till the moon has taken flight;
> To and fro we leap
> And chase the frothy bubbles,
> While the world is full of troubles
> And is anxious in its sleep.
> *Come away, O human child!*
> *To the waters and the wild*
> *With a faery, hand in hand,*
> *For the world's more full of weeping than you can understand.*[5]

[1] W. B. Yeats, *Collected Poems*, 1950, p. 14. Subsequent references to this volume are made as *CP*.

[2] *CP*, 279.   [3] *CP*, 7.   [4] *CP*, 9.   [5] *CP*, 20.

His interest in the popular ballad form, sustained intermittently to the end of his life, appeared in 'The Ballad of Father O'Hart'[1] and 'The Ballad of the Foxhunter',[2] the first giving literary life to the places where 'the mountains and the rivers and the roads became a possession of your life for ever', the second attempting to build upon an incident from a literary source, Kickham's *Knocknagow*, a novel well known in Ireland but probably still unheard of by most English readers. 'The Ballad of Moll Magee'[3] is mainly interesting as an early piece of characterisation based on a sermon delivered at Howth, then a fishing village outside Dublin. More successful is a memory of a snatch of song sung by an old woman at Ballisodare in Sligo which he made into 'Down by the Salley Gardens'.[4]

None of these poems, however, had fully released his imagination. He required the technique of symbolism for this: he needed the secrecy and the security that symbols would give him because he could hide his own insecurity behind them and could continue to remain, as it were, outside himself. Thus *The Wanderings of Oisin*,[5] his first long poem, contained several things which he did not want his readers to find out: 'they must not even know there is a symbol anywhere'. The poem is founded on various translations of Gaelic legends—Yeats himself never learned Gaelic—contained in the *Transactions of the Ossianic Society*, particularly Michael Comyn's eighteenth-century poem on the story of Oisin and Niamh.

As Yeats tells the story it lacks the toughness and directness of the original: we can get these qualities in Sir Samuel Ferguson's more direct handling of the Gaelic legends, in an epic rather than romantic manner. Though Yeats echoes the speed of Swinburne in his metre, though he owes something to Tennyson's Arthurianism (and his assonance) and though he is still steeped in Shelley he has arrived at material which can carry his own delicacy, his own detailed imagery and his preoccupation with the passing of time, the shortness of life and love. His inventiveness blends successfully with the Gaelic details in a tapestry-like picture, a new kind of poetry in which the Gaelic story is converted into a dreamy, cloudy beauty:

> Under the golden evening light,
> The immortals moved among the fountains
> By rivers and the woods' old night;

[1] *CP*, 23.   [2] *CP*, 27.   [3] *CP*, 25.   [4] *CP*, 22.   [5] *CP*, 409.

> Some danced like shadows on the mountains,
> Some wandered ever hand in hand;
> Or sat in dreams on the pale strand,
> Each forehead like an obscure star
> Bent down above each hookèd knee,
> And sang, and with a dreamy gaze
> Watched where the sun in a saffron blaze
> Was slumbering half in the sea-ways;
> And, as they sang, the painted birds
> Kept time with their bright wings and feet;
> Like drops of honey came their words,
> But fainter than a young lamb's bleat.[1]

The dream turns to nightmare in the second section of the poem, the Island of Victories, but the admixture of Coleridgean supernaturalism and Tennysonian lotus-eating is not as successful as the previous section, closer as it was to the concrete Gaelic originals:

> We galloped over the glossy sea:
> I know not if days passed or hours,
> And Niamh sang continually
> Danaan songs, and their dewy showers
> Of pensive laughter, unhuman sound,
> Lulled weariness, and softly round
> My human sorrow her white arms wound.
> We galloped; now a hornless deer
> Passed by us, chased by a phantom hound
> All pearly white, save one red ear;
> And now a lady rode like the wind
> With an apple of gold in her tossing hand;
> And a beautiful young man followed behind
> With quenchless gaze and fluttering hair.[2]

The symbolism was not very profound. The three islands of Living, of Victories, of Forgetfulness, may perhaps, as Ellmann suggests,[3] refer to Yeats's life in Sligo, London and Dublin. Oisin is a projection of aspects of his own life, and once he finished the poem he realised the symbolism needed interpretation. Though he could disguise his own incompleteness through the secrecy of such symbolism, he also saw virtues in the method

[1] *CP*, 421.   [2] *CP*, 413.
[3] R. Ellmann, *Yeats: the Man and the Masks*, 1949, p. 521.

because it was used by the mystical writers and poets he was beginning to admire fervently, and because it had a poetic validity of its own which had allowed him to break away from his early harmonious response to 'the more minute kinds of natural beauty' into a state of having something to say, however inarticulately.

2. *The Countess Cathleen*

Yeats was beginning to use a vocabulary freshly minted from the treasury of Gaelic literature, and many of the shorter poems in *The Countess Kathleen*[1] *and Various Legends and Lyrics* (1892) deal with a mythology Ireland had well nigh forgotten and England never known. For Arthur and his Round Table Yeats substituted the very different Conchubar and his Red Branch Warriors, and Finn and his Fenians. The Red Branch cycle of legends included Fergus, whom Ness had tricked out of his kingdom so that her son Conchubar could rule over Ulster in his stead, and in 'Fergus and the Druid' Yeats makes him avid for dreaming wisdom. Fergus was the unwitting agent of the doom of the Sons of Usna, Naoise the lover of Deirdre and his brothers Ardan and Ainle, who had accompanied the lovers to Scotland when they fled from Conchubar's wrath, for Deirdre was Conchubar's intended bride. Fergus had persuaded them to return against the wishes of Deirdre and had been tricked out of acting as their safe conduct. He joined with Maeve, Queen of Connaught, after this, in her raid on Ulster, in which Cuchulain achieved his great fame as Ulster's champion. Cuchulain is the Achilles of the Irish Saga, and he appears throughout Yeats's plays and poems, as warrior, as husband of Emer, as lover of Eithne Inguba, and of Aoife, as the unknowing killer of his own son and finally as victim of the sea.

In addition to drawing on the richness and strangeness of the saga material and making it part of his personal poetic language and mythology Yeats was carrying out his ambition of writing, like Allingham, poetry redolent of 'Munster grass and Connemara skies', about the places he knew in Ireland—Innisfree, Lissadell, Dromohair, Scanavin and Lugna-

---

[1] Yeats used an initial 'C' after 1895, and this spelling is subsequently used here except for one further reference to this particular volume.

Gall—and of transmitting, like the country story-tellers from whom he
had collected them, Irish fairy and folk tales. His rhymes were 'Danaan'
(after the Tuatha da Danaan, the legendary fairy folk who succeeded the
Milesian invaders of Ireland) and their scope had suddenly enlarged. He
had written *The Wanderings of Oisin* in 1887, the year his father moved
his family back to London again; it was published in 1889, in the spring
of which year Maud Gonne came into his life and he fell in love with
her:

> I had never thought to see in a living woman so great beauty. It
> belonged to famous pictures, to poetry, to some legendary past. A
> complexion like the bloom of apples and yet the face and body had
> the beauty of lineaments which Blake calls the highest beauty because
> it changes least from youth to age, and stature so great that she seemed
> of a divine race. Her movements were works of grace and I under-
> stood at last why the poets of antiquity, where we could but speak of
> face and form, sing, serving some lady, that she seems like a goddess.[1]

She was the incarnation of the Shelleyan heroines who had filled his
dreams, wild and beautiful. He did not speak of love and intended not
to, but he could offer poetic devotion in defeatist adoration. Maud is
his Helen and his Deirdre:

> Who dreamed that beauty passes like a dream?
> For these red lips, with all their mournful pride,
> Mournful that no new wonder may betide,
> Troy passed away in one high funeral gleam,
> And Usna's children died.[2]

This devotion follows upon the Thoreau-like dream of living a solitary life
on an island in Lough Gill, Sligo, a dream immortalised in 'The Lake Isle of
Innisfree',[3] a poem inspired by home-sickness in London for the scenery
of Sligo. It became his best-known early poem, an anthology piece
which celebrates the loneliness of adolescence. His poems now begin to
deal with the pity and sorrow of love; he wishes he and Maud Gonne
(for she is the 'beloved' of these poems) were white birds; he dreams of
her death and carves a tribute to her beauty on a cross above her grave;
he alone loved her pilgrim soul. This is sad, pre-Raphaelite devotion:
'What wife would she make, I thought, what share could she have in the

[1] W. B. Yeats, *Unpublished Autobiography*.
[2] 'The Rose of the World', *CP*, 41.   [3] *CP*, 44.

life of a student?' Shortage of money was indeed a hindrance (he was extremely poor until he was about forty); but in 1891 he asked her to marry him and was refused; he continued to propose to her at intervals and was always told that they should not marry but remain friends.[1]

It was to impress Maud Gonne that he offered to write *The Countess Cathleen* based on a story he had come across while collecting material for his *Fairy and Folk Tales of the Irish Peasantry* (1888); this was to be a play in which she could act the role of the Countess who is tempted to sell her soul to provide food for her peasants in a famine. Yeats wanted to convince Maud Gonne of his ability to play a public part, a popular part in the movement for Irish independence, to which she had given herself with fantastic zeal. But he also wrote the play as a warning to her that she was in danger of losing her own soul through this immersion in political activity. His role, he thought, was to reshape Ireland's literature, an aim deliberately put in 'To Ireland in the Coming Times':

> Know, that I would accounted be
> True brother of a company
> That sang, to sweeten Ireland's wrong,
> Ballad and story, rann and song.[2]

His patriotic impulse was different from that of the nineteenth-century Irish nationalist poets, as this poem makes clear:

> Nor may I less be counted one
> With Davis, Mangan, Ferguson,
> Because, to him who ponders well,
> My rhymes more than their rhyming tell
> Of things discovered in the deep,
> Where only body's laid asleep.

His rhymes carried more than their surface meaning because he had begun to add to the local descriptions and Gaelic material a symbolism which he had been learning through his steadily increasing interest in the mystics, in heterodox religion, in the occult, in Rosicrucianism, in Theosophy and in magic. This had begun in his teens in Dublin when he sought authority for his thesis that legends, beliefs and emotions handed on by poets, painters, philosophers and theologians are the nearest approach we have to truth.

[1] See J. Hone *W. B. Yeats 1865–1939*, 1942, pp. 84, 111, 124 and 194, and A. Norman Jeffares, *W. B. Yeats: Man and Poet*, 1949, pp. 39 and 40.
[2] *CP*, 56.

From reading A. P. Sinnett's *Esoteric Buddhism* it had been an easy step to form the Hermetic Society in order to discuss Theosophy and Oriental religion generally. After that he had joined the Dublin Theosophical Lodge. In London he had subsequently found a sage in Madame Blavatsky and was admitted to the Esoteric Section of the Theosophical Society. There his desire for experiment—his wish to believe was mingled with a healthy scepticism—had resulted in a request that he should resign. Then he discovered a magician, the author of *The Kabbalah Unveiled*, MacGregor Mathers, through whom he joined the Order of the Golden Dawn. This was a society of Christian cabbalists through which he learned a good deal about alchemy. His interest in the *Kabbalah* (these are Hebrew writings treasured by occultists since the Middle Ages, which blend cosmogony with explanations of Biblical material) led him to collaborate with Edwin Ellis in an explanation of Blake's symbolism which resulted in the publication of a three volume edition of Blake's works 'Poetic, symbolic and critical' in 1893. This contained an interpretation and paraphrased commentary, and Blake's ideas and his private language continued to have a strong effect on Yeats's practice.

Partly because of his belief that poetry should consist of essences, partly because of his innate liking for mystery and secrecy, partly because he was still feeling his way into a symbolist technique, many of the poems included in *The Countess Kathleen* (first grouped together under *The Rose* in *Poems* of 1895) are still decorative in effect. But Yeats was using the symbol of the rose to carry an increasingly complex meaning. The Rose stood for Ireland in the work of several Irish poets; it had, of course, its traditional meanings in the work of contemporary English poets, though some of them were extending the range of these meanings; the conjunction of four-petalled rose and cross was fundamental in the Rosicrucian system, and symbolised a fifth element, a mystic marriage—the rose being a feminine symbol, the cross masculine. The rose also symbolised spiritual beauty, an idea derived from Blake; in 'To the Rose upon the Rood of Time'[1] the rose is eternal beauty. And it also symbolised Maud Gonne's beauty and, again through her, Ireland.

'The Two Trees',[2] however, is more esoteric than any of the Rose poems; it marks the beginning of Yeats's increasingly dramatic use of the opposites of subjectivity and objectivity; it draws upon the Kabbalistic tradition, and its trees bear an obvious relationship to the Tree of Life and the Tree of Knowledge of Biblical tradition; and, of course, as Yeats

[1] *CP*, 35.   [2] *CP*, 54.

tells us himself, to Blake. The elements from Blake have been well explained by Professor Kermode,[1] and Dr. F. A. C. Wilson has written an elaborate exegesis of the poem, relating it with an instinctive rather than authoritative reconstruction to Yeats's working 'backwards from Blake to Blake's sources in myth'.[2] What we see, however, is the poem, and if it is to be judged successful it must act on us as a poem *per se*. The beauty or the menace of an iceberg should be obvious without the experts' information about the five-sixths invisible under the surface. It is very useful indeed to know of the existence of the subsurface meaning if we are to comprehend the totality of a complex symbolic poem, but we must beware of critics aqualunged with inspiration who may spend so much time in the depths that we forget we are concerned with the poetry. 'The Two Trees', for instance, works without our knowing about the Kabbalistic Tree; it was meant to do so. We can recognise the symbolic value of the tree image implicitly without Yeats's particular insistence on its archetypal meaning; we realise, as he intended us to, its affirmative and negative values as we get to know the whole of his poetry because, as he continued to make his way into his own symbolic technique, he learned from Shelley's habit of continually repeating symbols. The poems in *The Rose* do not attain the power of those written subsequently because the process of establishing symbolic meaning must be cumulative. (This is where Dr. Wilson's explanations, extremely enlightening as they often are, sometimes mislead, because he has no evidence that Yeats's meanings were initially as explicit, as cut and dried, or as complex as he is able, through critical hindsight, to make them appear.) Yeats had to push his work further than an art for art's sake theory of poetry: literature had, for him, to have conviction. A symbol,' he wrote in an essay on Blake, 'is indeed the only possible expression of some invisible essence', and again, after describing how he lost the desire of describing outward things, took little pleasure in books unless they were 'spiritual and unemphatic', and came to realise that his change of attitude was part of a large movement of European thought, he wrote in 'The Autumn of the Body':

> The arts are, I believe, about to take about their shoulders the burdens that have fallen from the shoulders of the priests, and to lead us back upon our journey by filling our thoughts with the essence of

[1] F. Kermode, *Romantic Image*, 1957, p. 96.
[2] F. A. C. Wilson, *Yeats's Iconography*, 1960, p. 251.

things, and not with things. We are about to substitute once more the distillation of alchemy for the analyses of chemistry and for some other sciences; and certain of us are looking everywhere for the perfect alembic that no silver or golden drop may escape.

He thought that

the more a poet rids his verses of heterogeneous knowledge and irrelevant analysis, and purifies his mind with elaborate art, the more does the little ritual of his verse resemble the great ritual of Nature, and become mysterious and inscrutable.

3. The Wind Among the Reeds

Yeats's own poetry became more refined and more complex. He had learnt elaboration from Wilde and Pater. His technique benefited by discussions with poets of the nineties, the craftsmen who were members of the Rhymers' Club, in the founding of which Yeats played a major part in 1891. Its members, whom Yeats described later as 'the Tragic Generation', included Lionel Johnson, Ernest Dowson, John Davidson, Richard de Gallienne, Ernest Rhys, Arthur Symons and others. They all admired pre-Raphaelite work, especially that of Rossetti and Pater, and they met regularly to discuss literature in the upper room of 'The Cheshire Cheese', an ancient eating house in Fleet Street. But it was Arthur Symons who taught him most; he introduced him to the practice and the ideas of the French Symbolist poets. From the examples of Villiers de L'Isle Adam, Maeterlinck and Mallarmé he formed an idea of a more select audience, to which he addressed most of the poems of *The Wind Among the Reeds* (1899).

Though *The Wind Among the Reeds* contains such simple, ballad style poems as 'The Host of the Air'[1] and such deceptively simple, gay, lilting lyrics as 'The Fiddler of Dooney',[2] the majority are far from the style of his first poems, all that he had copied from the folk art of Ireland. As he wrote the Rose poems he thought he was becoming unintelligible to the young men who had been in his thought, but he continued to move farther in the direction of a 'pure' poetry, which does not reflect

[1] *CP*, 63.   [2] *CP*, 82.

his own increasingly more complicated life. As he became more actively engaged in affairs a weariness descended on his poetry, in part prompted by the unsatisfactory nature of his love affair. His proposals of marriage to Maud met with no success, and his aims for regenerating Irish literature did not fully interest her, as hers were entirely political. After Parnell's death in 1891 Yeats founded two literary societies, but in three years it was obvious that he would not be able to get his own way with the schemes for new publications which he had successfully initiated. He turned his attention to the possibility of the theatre, but in 1896 he joined the secret extremist Irish Republican Brotherhood (or I.R.B.), and became preoccupied for two years with an attempt to unite all the Irish political parties under the umbrella of an association for the celebration of the centenary of the '98 Rebellion and its leader Wolfe Tone.

None of this activity could be guessed at from his poems. He was apparently taking very seriously an idea of creating a Celtic Order of Mysteries, a blend of his nationalism and his preoccupation with hetero-dox doctrines and rituals. Maud Gonne was involved in his plans, which involved the use of a deserted castle in Lough Kay in Roscommon. The business of drafting the rites of this order went on for a time with the help of MacGregor Mathers, who was finally thrown out of the Order of the Golden Dawn in 1900. Part of Yeats's interest in this idea lay in the possibility of turning Maud Gonne from her active politics—the riots which occurred in Dublin after a speech of hers had alarmed as well as excited Yeats—and remnants of his quietism and the Innisfree escapism survive in the poems of the nineties:

The wrong of unshapely things is a wrong too great to be told;
I hunger to build them anew and sit on a green knoll apart,
With the earth and the sky and the water, re-made, like a casket of gold
For my dreams of your image that blossoms a rose in the deeps of my
    heart.[1]

The most successful of his symbolist poems of the nineties are those which use the imagery of Gaelic poems. 'The Song of Wandering Aengus',[2] for instance, has more precision and is less vague in its effect than poems such as 'The Unappeasable Host'[3] or 'He bids his beloved be at peace'.[4] But in nearly all the poems of *The Wind Among the Reeds*

---

[1] 'The Lover tells of the Rose in his Heart', *CP*, 62.
[2] *CP*, 66.   [3] *CP*, 65.   [4] *CP*, 69.

the twilight is too deep, the passion too dim, and even in 'He remembers forgotten beauty'[1]—which Joyce seized on as typical of Yeats at this period—the poetry is too dream-heavy with incantatory qualities to seem more than a wearied swoon. Here are some of the 'passion-dimmed' words which mute the tone of this adjectival poetry: pale, paling, cloud-pale, death-pale, pearl-pale, desolate, dim, dream-dimmed, dove-grey, drowsy, love-lorn, vain, defeated, faint, piteous, glimmering, grey, passion-dimmed, shadowy, trembling, still.

Yet the volume is not unattractive. 'The Song of Wandering Aengus' draws strength from its nouns, its deliberate repetitions and its use of stronger verbs than usual—peeled, hooked, dropped:

> I went out to the hazel wood,
> Because a fire was in my head,
> And cut and peeled a hazel wand,
> And hooked a berry to a thread;
> And when white moths were on the wing,
> And moth-like stars were flickering out,
> I dropped the berry in a stream
> And caught a little silver trout.[2]

The poem, derived, according to Yeats, from a Greek folk song, is a dream of successful love, the triumphant conclusion gaining strength from its symbolism, for the 'silver apples of the moon / The golden apples of the sun' probably come from 'a comment of MacGregor Mathers' that the Tree of Life in Kabbalistic lore is an apple tree with sun and moon for fruit. This symbolism links up with the glimmering girl 'with apple blossom in her hair' (an image of Maud Gonne repeated later in 'The Arrow'),[3] and it is also repeating the 'apple of gold' used in *The Wanderings of Oisin* and there taken from the precise imagery of the Gaelic original. This kind of complex relationship between symbols was to be used by Yeats with increasing richness of suggestion and meaning.

There are a number of poems carrying the early melancholia of his teens, now transmuted into vain longing for his beloved in 'He hears the Cry of the Sedge',[4] 'He reproves the Curlew'[5] and 'He wishes his beloved were dead',[6] and into a curiously aged weariness in 'The Everlasting Voices'[7] and 'Into the Twilight',[8] which deals with an 'outworn heart, in a time outworn.' There are poems in which he cele-

[1] *CP*, 69.   [2] *CP*, 66.   [3] *CP*, 85.   [4] *CP*, 75.
[5] *CP*, 69.   [6] *CP*, 80.   [7] *CP*, 61.   [8] *CP*, 65.

brates Maud's beauty: 'He tells of the perfect beauty',[1] 'He tells of a valley full of lovers',[2] 'He thinks of those who have spoken evil of his beloved'.[3] These poems look ahead to a posthumous situation and they come perilously near to mere attitudinising. This is avoided by 'The Lover asks forgiveness because of his many moods',[4] which unfolds, tapestry-like, mingled strands of pre-Raphaelite romanticism, Gaelic material and unhappy love which Yeats shot through with his mystical symbolism and with touches of modish ninety-ish decadence.

'The Secret Rose'[5] has a series of incantatory cadences which create emotive intensity. A similar series is also used in 'He thinks of his Past Greatness when a Part of the Constellations of Heaven',[6] but 'Red Hanrahan's Song about Ireland'[7] is more successful in this kind of slow movement; it swirls sound around in its hymnal of Maud Gonne and Ireland. The supreme cry, however, of Yeats's idealised devotion is 'He wishes for the Cloths of Heaven'.[8] This is the poetry of the half-light at its best, genuinely gentle, and achieving its *cri de cœur* by moving from rich elaboration into an arresting simplicity:

> Had I the heavens' embroidered cloths,
> Enwrought with golden and silver light,
> The blue and the dim and the dark cloths
> Of night and light and the half-light,
> I would spread the cloths under your feet:
> But I, being poor, have only my dreams;
> I have spread my dreams under your feet;
> Tread softly because you tread on my dreams.

4. In the Seven Woods

The Wind Among the Reeds had carried Yeats's thesis of romantic devotion and poetry of essences, of beauty and implicit mysteries to high water mark. Signs of withdrawal are visible in some of the poems of *In the Seven Woods* (1904). Though the decorative element survives in 'Under the Moon',[9] now his dreaming 'of women whose beauty was folded in dismay/Even in an old story, is a burden not to be borne'.

[1] *CP*, 74. [2] *CP*, 74. [3] *CP*, 75. [4] *CP*, 73. [5] *CP*, 77.
[6] *CP*, 81. [7] *CP*, 90. [8] *CP*, 81. [9] *CP*, 91.

The 'old high way of love'[1] has created weariness in the heart, and the 'well-belovèd's hair has threads of grey'.[2]

An earlier poem, 'The lover mourns for the loss of love,' was probably as realistic in its biographical basis; it could well describe the one brief interlude in Yeats's love since he was twenty-three. He had a brief affair when he was thirty-one with 'Diana Vernon', a married woman, but this did not overcome his preoccupation with Maud Gonne:

> I had a beautiful friend
> And dreamed that the old despair
> Would end in love in the end:
> She looked in my heart one day
> And saw your image was there;
> She has gone weeping away.[3]

His unrequited devotion to Maud continued. Though his proposals of marriage were declined, he found his friendship rewarding. Though he travelled with her to meetings in England and Scotland, speaking of the aims of the '98 Association, he still hoped to persuade her to leave politics, marry him and share a life of spiritual quietude. He still shared with her his dream of recreating an heroic Ireland through a Celtic Order of Mysteries, of establishing the Castle of Heroes in Lough Kay. When they both left the Irish Republican Brotherhood she turned her attention to Arthur Griffith's Sinn Fein movement, but failed to interest Yeats in it. He was involved in the expulsion of MacGregor Mathers from the Order of the Golden Dawn and in the creation of another magical order.

In 1896 Yeats first met Lady Gregory; the following year he paid the first of many long visits to Coole Park, her house in Galway. For him this was a vitalising experience for in Coole Park he found—

what I had been seeking always, a life of order, and of labour, where all outward things were the image of an inward life . . . here many generations, and no uncultured generations, had left the images of their service in furniture, in statues, in pictures and in the outline of wood and field. I think I was not born for a master but for a servant and that it has been my unhappiness to see the analytical faculty dissolve all those things that meant our service, and so it is that all images of service are dear to me.[4]

[1] 'Adam's Curse', CP, 88.
[2] 'The Folly of Being Comforted', CP, 86.   [3] CP, 68.
[4] W. B. Yeats, Unpublished Autobiography.

Yeats had already experienced some of the pleasure of life in an Irish country house when he visited the Gore-Booths at Lissadell (that old Georgian mansion of 'In Memory of Eva Gore-Booth and Con Markiewicz')[1] in 1896, but now he saw himself in the role of a Renaissance courtier, an idea developed later in poems such as 'These are the Clouds',[2] 'Upon a House Shaken by the Land Agitation',[3] 'The People',[4] 'The New Faces',[5] and later in 'Coole Park, 1929'[6] and 'Coole Park and Ballylee, 1931',[7] which look back upon the role of the house and its mistress in the Irish Renaissance. Coole was a place of custom and ceremony; a routine gently imposed by Lady Gregory made Coole at once his 'place of industry' as well as a place where life moved 'within restraint through gracious forms'. He had found here the embodiment of Lionel Johnson's saying that life should be a ritual. Aristocratic order, the ideal of tragic gaiety, of dignity, the attitude of 'Cast a cold eye / On life, on death,'[8] even the formality of the dance were, for Yeats, centred in reality upon Coole, in idealistic imagining upon Byzantium. Though his family had its history, it was part of the small gentry of Ireland and had not provided him with visible images of inherited culture. His artistic independence (which was originally nourished on his father's belief that a gentleman should not be concerned with 'getting on') encouraged him to scorn bourgeois society and bourgeois values, to set above them images of aristocratic life, or below them the world of beggarmen. Ireland provided him with both extremes.

Yeats came increasingly to contrast aristocratic ideals of private culture and public service with those of the revolutionaries. His attempt to impose unity on the Nationalistic movement in 1897 and 1898 and his experiences of the Irish Republican Brotherhood left him dissatisfied and disillusioned with political life; his literary movement had not progressed as he had wished, and yet by 1898 he was 'very full of play-writing'. His friendship with Lady Gregory led him to believe that it might actually be possible to bring an Irish theatre into being. He threw himself wholeheartedly into this task, working closely with Edward Martyn and George Moore as well as Lady Gregory. With them he was a co-director of the Irish Literary Theatre and this, by 1902, had become the Irish National Dramatic Society, with Yeats as its president.

The Countess Cathleen was put on in 1899, and in 1902 Maud Gonne

[1] *CP*, 263.   [2] *CP*, 107.   [3] *CP*, 106.   [4] *CP*, 169.
[5] *CP*, 238.   [6] *CP*, 273.   [7] *CP*, 275.
[8] 'Under Ben Bulben', *CP*, 397.

appeared in the title role of *Cathleen ni Houlihan*. This play had an elec-
trifying effect on its audience as Stephen Gwynn has recorded:

> I went home asking myself if such plays should be produced unless
> one was prepared for people to go out and shoot and be shot. Yeats
> was not alone responsible; no doubt but Lady Gregory had helped
> him to get the peasant speech so perfect; but above all Miss Gonne's
> impersonation had stirred the audience as I have never seen another
> audience stirred.[1]

And Yeats wondered in his old age: 'Did that play of mine send out /
Certain men the English shot?'[2] In 1904 the Abbey Theatre opened with
Yeats as Production Manager, and the following year Lady Gregory,
Synge and he were co-directors of a limited company replacing the
previous organisation. He was now fully engaged in 'Theatre business,
management of men'.[3]

5. *The Green Helmet*

In 1903 Maud Gonne suddenly, without warning, married John
MacBride. Yeats was deeply hurt, and resentful. He wrote in his
Diary:

> My dear is angry, that of late
> I cry all base blood down
> As if she had not taught me hate
> By kisses to a clown.[4]

He had always wanted marriage, and now, at thirty-seven, he seemed to
have wasted his dreams on a barren passion:

> But O, in a minute she changed—
> O, do not love too long,
> Or you will grow out of fashion
> Like an old song.[5]

[1] Stephen Gwynn, *Irish Literature and Drama*, 1936, p. 158.
[2] 'The Man and the Echo', *CP*, 393.
[3] 'The Fascination of What's Difficult', *CP*, 104.
[4] Jeffares, 142.   [5] 'O do not Love too long', *CP*, 93.

All he could do was celebrate her beauty in poems like 'Peace',[1] looking
back on the past in discerning poems like 'Words'[2] or 'Against un-
worthy Praise',[3] in magnificent poems like 'No Second Troy',[4] where
after retailing with dignity the misery she had caused him, and the
revolutionary violence she had preached, he finally equates her with
Helen and so excuses all:

> Why, what could she have done, being what she is?
> Was there another Troy for her to burn?

The simplicity achieved in these poems is part of his new attitude to
writing:

> Through all the lying days of my youth
> I swayed my leaves and flowers in the sun;
> Now I may wither into the truth.[5]

He reacted violently against the ideas he had put forward up to 1899; his
new work seems the antithesis of all he had written before.

These poems express Yeats's personal disillusionment with love; but
there were other literary factors at work which were changing his attitude to style. In *The Seven Woods* he had two obliquely direct references
to contemporary events; the next volume, *The Green Helmet*, refers
directly to the Abbey Theatre, Galway Races, Dublin students, Coole,
and its flat statement paves the way for the poetry of *Responsibilities*, the
full antithesis of the twilight. The range of his poetry widens in *The
Green Helmet*, though for some years after 1903 he wrote little poetry.
All things could tempt him from his craft of verse; and 'The Fascination of What's Difficult' gives us some of the reasons:

> . . . My curse on plays
> That have to be set up in fifty ways,
> On the day's war with every knave and dolt . . .[6]

6. *Responsibilities*

Yeats had reached another stage of his development. In his political
activities of the nineties he had, he wrote later, surrendered to the chief

[1] *CP*, 103.   [2] *CP*, 100.   [3] *CP*, 103.   [4] *CP*, 101.
[5] 'The Coming of Wisdom with Time', *CP*, 105.   [6] *CP*, 104.

temptation of the artist—creation without toil. Now he was involved in a most unselfish labour, working ultimately to provide a stage for realistic plays whose writers' aims were different from his own dreams for a poetic drama. Already disconcerted by learning what mob violence meant, when Maud Gonne would 'Have taught to ignorant men most violent ways',[1] already disturbed by finding the politicians among whom he had tried to work ineffective and small minded, he made the bitter discovery that the Irish public disliked the great art he was attempting to create and foster by his unselfish public service. For this period of work at the Abbey was inspired by his new knowledge of the enlightened patronage under which artistic creation flourished in Renaissance Italy.

Yeats shared with Lady Gregory and Synge a desire for 'vivid and beautiful language' which would help him in his attempts to prune staging to a minimum, to remove movement from acting. His initial impulse was to write for an audience of countrymen and artisans. His journey to Italy with Lady Gregory in 1907, his summer visits to Coole, strengthened his belief in aristocratic values and peasant vitality. He was to reject the middle classes and despise the city mob pugnaciously during two public controversies; he was to show his full emergence from the twilight of aestheticism by writing polemical poems full of passionate rhetoric and sardonic directness.

These controversies revolved round art. The first arose when some of the audience demonstrated against Synge's *The Playboy of the Western World* on its first night in 1907. Yeats had had the same kind of trouble over his own play *The Countess Cathleen* some years earlier, but this new outburst of chauvinistic philistinism seemed to attack all his plans for moulding a new cultural outlook in Ireland; he fought successfully for Synge's play, but began to think his 'blind bitter land' was so twisted by political hatred that it could appreciate neither literature nor art. 'On Those That Hated "The Playboy of the Western World", 1907'[2] makes clear a new scorn of the public, a sinewy economy of style. The controversy over the Lane pictures, however, produced in his poetry for the first time some of the rank fruit of his political experiences. The very title, 'To a wealthy man who promised a second subscription to the Dublin Municipal Gallery if it were proved the people wanted pictures',[3] sets the tone of the poem in advance. Political rhetoric motivates the poem, contrasting those ideal patrons of the past, Duke Ercole, Guido-

[1] 'No Second Troy', *CP*, 101.   [2] *CP*, 124.   [3] *CP*, 119.

baldo and Cosimo with Dublin's 'wealthy man' and comparing the 'blind and ignorant' town of Dublin with Urbino, 'that Grammar School of courtesies', of which he had read in Castiglione's *Book of the Courtier* (another poem 'The People'[1] makes masterly use of an incident in this book) and which he had visited with all the awed delight that lovely hill town, and architecturally perfect palace richly deserve. These contrasts continue in 'September 1913',[2] where contemporary praying and saving make 'Romantic Ireland' seem dead and gone and with his heroic mentor, O'Leary, in the grave.

In the midst of his grief and scorn Yeats is beginning to build a new set of symbols. He is adding to his earlier 'Davis, Mangan, Ferguson' both O'Leary and Parnell. 'To a Shade'[3] is tentatively adding Sir Hugh Lane to their ranks, though not as yet by name, for he was still alive as Yeats was writing the poem. He had offered his superb collection of paintings as a gift to the Dublin Corporation on condition that they were suitably housed. But, like Parnell, he seems to Yeats a man of 'passionate serving kind' who must suffer at the hands of the ignorant, of the 'fumbling wits, the obscure spite' of the Paudeens.

'To a Shade' deserves careful examination: it is superbly wrought, its tone controlled, its architectonic quality marked. Its supercharging of meaning is two-staged; the poet addresses the dead patriot's ghost in order to display the detestability of Dublin's philistines. Parnell's ghost is given the choice of visiting his monument or the ghostly splendours of eighteenth-century houses along the quays, and advised to leave because 'they are at their old tricks yet'. The hint of Parnell's fate at the hands of his countrymen (later elaborated in 'Parnell's Funeral')[4] is caught up in the second stanza. The ideal of service is spurned by these men, and a man who has brought benefits is, like Parnell, 'driven from the place'. The stanza rises to passionate scorn and links Parnell and Lane; their common enemy 'an old foul mouth' has led the hunt. The ending of the second stanza picks up and explains the 'old tricks' of the first; now the last stanza rounds off the opening image of Parnell's memory— the monument at the end of O'Connell Street—by referring to his burial place at Glasnevin Cemetery, and then catches up the image of Dublin's beauty by saying the time has not come for him to taste of the 'salt breath' before delivering its final satiric thrust, that he is safer in the tomb than in the Dublin which has heaped insult upon Lane, for he has 'had enough of sorrow before death'.

[1] *CP*, 169.   [2] *CP*, 120.   [3] *CP*, 123.   [4] *CP*, 319.

The poem blends formality with colloquialism, rhetoric with remark ('I wonder if the builder has been paid'); its imagery is economical yet evocative; and its intertwining of the treatment of the two men subtle and sophisticated. The beauty of Dublin (the 'grey Eighteenth-century houses' of 'Easter 1916'[1] gain ironic meaning when referred back to this poem) stands as a constant image against which the ugliness of 'the pack' can be measured; the 'old tricks' echo through the 'old foul mouth', but both are summed up in the results of their actions upon others in the last stanza's 'sorrow'. The aristocratic ideal of unselfish service is sketched in passionately yet entirely unsentimentally: its demands are passion, full hands, pains; its rewards may be disgrace and sorrow. The sorrow is, ultimately, the poet's as well as that of Lane and Parnell, but the real disgrace is Dublin's; and, ultimately, it is the pack which suffers the loss in its children's children of—

> loftier thought,
> Sweeter emotion, working in their veins
> Like gentle blood. . . .

Though the demands are rigorous and the rewards saddening, there may yet be compensation for the men of 'passionate serving kind'. 'To a friend whose work has come to nothing',[2] a poem written to Lady Gregory who was working hard on behalf of the Lane plan (he was her nephew), suggests that the private values of secrecy and exultant pride outweigh the brazen threats and all the obscure spite, the insults and disgrace which are the public response to generosity and 'What the exultant heart calls good'.

These poems have the breathless tempo of angry speech: they argue; they put rhetorical questions; and they are effectively colloquial. Though their verbs are simpler and stronger than before, the force of the poems come from nouns and adjectives. The colloquial element becomes conversational in 'The Three Beggars'[3] and 'The Three Hermits',[4] both of which bring out Yeats's idiosyncratic invention of symbolic characters. This speech is stylised into Yeats's idiom in 'Beggar to Beggar Cried',[5] 'Running to Paradise'[6] and 'The Hour before Dawn'.[7] The last poem has some points of technique which are to be developed further in later poems. The Rossetti-like 'attack' of the poem, for instance, acts like a stage direction:

[1] *CP*, 202.   [2] *CP*, 122.   [3] *CP*, 124.   [4] *CP*, 127.
[5] *CP*, 128.   [6] *CP*, 129.   [7] *CP*, 130.

> A cursing rogue with a merry face
> A bundle of rags upon a crutch
> Stumbled upon that windy plain
> Called Cruachan . . .

Here also are new verbal nuances which are to become more familiar: the use of 'but' in 'If he but stayed' or 'And there's no man but cocks his ear'; the use of the present participle 'Being certain it was no right work'; the use of 'O' in the cry 'O would 'twere spring'; of 'for' meaning 'in spite of' or 'because of' in 'I should not be too down in the mouth / For anything you did or said'.

Many of these locutions are simply turns of Anglo-Irish speech and indicate a great confidence on Yeats's part; he had 'learned his trade' with the English poets, his 'companions of The Cheshire Cheese', and now he knew when to go beyond conventions or fashions and impose his own usages upon his poems. Ezra Pound may have influenced the harsh outspokenness of these poems, in which Yeats is using beggar men and tramps as foils to his heroic figures; this directness of speech possibly derives from his increasing practice in the writing of plays. The heroic qualities of Cuchulain, for instance, are brought out in contrast with the Blind Man and the Fool in *On Baile's Strand* (1903). And the characters in the plays owe much to Synge's work—as a poem 'The Dolls'[1] probably derives from a passage in Synge's *The Aran Isles*. In subject matter Yeats was now permitting himself a far wider range: there was room for his own sardonic humour in 'The Scholars'[2] (the original version under Pound's influence was stronger) and 'An Appointment',[3] where the final lines carry an epigrammatic terseness. This movement from the quiet cadences of the twilight poems is another mark of confidence—and skill; the final lines now sum up the poems and give them an epigrammatic quality. They are what we remember: 'Was there another Troy for her to burn?'; 'I might have thrown poor words away / And been content to live'; 'No government appointed him'; 'And I may dine at journey's end / With Landor and with Donne'; 'Lord, what would they say / Did their Catullus walk that way?'

Yeats later wrote that at the end of the century 'we all got down off our stilts', and his adoption of new attitudes and styles was part of a sound literary instinct. He realised that he had carried the Celtic imagery as far as he could:

[1] *CP*, 141.　　　[2] *CP*, 158.　　　[3] *CP*, 141.

I made my song a coat
Covered with embroideries
Out of old mythologies
From heel to throat;
But the fools caught it,
Wore it in the world's eyes
As though they'd wrought it.
Song, let them take it,
For there's more enterprise
In walking naked.[1]

This new poetic nakedness involved the stripping of illusion, and 'The Fisherman' does this to anything that might have been left of Yeats's idealistic ambitions—'What I had hoped 'twould be / To write for my own race'—by contrasting them with the reality:

The living men that I hate,
The dead man that I loved,
The craven man in his seat,
The insolent unreproved,
And no knave brought to book
Who has won a drunken cheer,
The witty man and his joke
Aimed at the commonest ear,
The clever man who cries
The catch-cries of the clown,
The beating down of the wise
And great Art beaten down.[2]

In addition to the disillusionment caused him by revolutionary mobs and bourgeois philistines, there was hatred evoked by the malice of George Moore, who had referred in *Hail and Farewell* to Yeats's family background. He came from the professional class of Anglo-Irish (English notions of class structure cannot easily or effectively be applied to Ireland)—his ancestors being merchants and clergy; and now he became interested in his family history. He began to elevate his ancestors into his personal mythology, to be as expansive in delineating details as in proffering proper names. The prologue to *Responsibilities*[3] and 'In Memory of Alfred Pollexfen'[4] dignify his relatives and focus attention

---

[1] 'A Coat', *CP*, 142.   [2] *CP*, 166.
[3] 'Introductory Rhymes', *CP*, 113.   [4] *CP*, 175.

upon them as personalities interesting in their own right as well as being part of his family. But he realised poignantly that he had not played his proper part in continuing this family history:

> Pardon that for a barren passion's sake,
> Although I have come close on forty-nine,
> I have no child, I have nothing but a book,
> Nothing but that to prove your blood and mine.[1]

This barren passion preoccupied him still; after Maud Gonne had separated from John MacBride in 1905, Yeats and she resumed their friendship, and he continued to write love poetry about her with the elegiac note that had appeared in *The Green Helmet*, celebrating past memories 'When age might well have chilled his blood' in such poems as 'A Memory of Youth',[2] 'Fallen Majesty',[3] 'Friends',[4] 'That the Night Come',[5] 'Memory',[6] 'Her Praise',[7] 'The People',[8] 'His Phoenix',[9] 'A Thought from Propertius',[10] 'Broken Dreams',[11] 'A Deep-Sworn Vow'[12] and 'Presences'.[13] These poems have a dignity about them which comes from their concentration upon the object of his love. Small details, memories of conversations or scenes give these poems convincing reality; they are obviously the work of a man who 'gave all his heart and lost', yet none of them matches the wildly passionate outcry of 'The Cold Heaven', metaphysical in its mixture of blood and spirit, its tense questioning, its evocation of mood:

> Suddenly I saw the cold and rook-delighting heaven
> That seemed as though ice burned and was but the more ice,
> And thereupon imagination and heart were driven
> So wild that every casual thought of that and this
> Vanished, and left but memories, that should be out of season
> With the hot blood of youth, of love crossed long ago;
> Until I cried and trembled and rocked to and fro,
> Riddled with light. Ah! When the ghost begins to quicken,
> Confusion of the death bed over, is it sent
> Out naked on the roads, as the books say, and stricken
> By the injustice of the skies for punishment?[14]

[1] *CP*, 113.   [2] *CP*, 137.   [3] *CP*, 138.   [4] *CP*, 139.
[5] *CP*, 140.   [6] *CP*, 168.   [7] *CP*, 168.   [8] *CP*, 169.
[9] *CP*, 170.   [10] *CP*, 172.   [11] *CP*, 172.   [12] *CP*, 174.
[13] *CP*, 174.   [14] *CP*, 140.

Yeats had experienced both vicariously and personally

> The daily spite of this unmannerly town,
> Where who has served the most is most defamed,
> The reputation of his life time lost
> Between the night and morning.[1]

He had gone through the purgation of being misunderstood, of having his motives impugned, but there was still more to experience, the realisation that he had himself misjudged others. The 1916 Rebellion took him by surprise:

> I have met them at close of day
> Coming with vivid faces
> From counter or desk among grey
> Eighteenth-century houses.
> I have passed with a nod of the head
> Or polite meaningless words,
> Or have lingered a while and said
> Polite meaningless words,
> And thought before I had done
> Of a mocking tale or a gibe
> To please a companion
> Around the fire at the club,
> Being certain that they and I
> But lived where motley is worn:
> All changed, changed utterly:
> A terrible beauty is born.[2]

Though 'Easter 1916' recants Yeats's belief that the revolutionaries would never do anything, he wrote to Lady Gregory at the time that all the work of years had been overturned. After his experience of the heights of public life in the nineties, when it seemed he might become the man of the hour, the 1916 Rebellion appeared at once tragic in itself and something from which he had been excluded and had excluded himself. But just as Maud Gonne's marriage in 1903 had sent his dreams crashing, the execution of MacBride as one of the leaders of the Rising brought about some of the events which contributed to the great change in Yeats as poet.

[1] 'The People', CP, 169.   [2] 'Easter 1918', CP, 202.

7. The Wild Swans at Coole

In the summer of 1916 Yeats went to France, where Maud Gonne was acting as a nurse in Normandy. Once more he proposed marriage to her, was refused, and then began to envisage marriage to her adopted daughter Iseult Gonne. The disparity in age troubled him:

> . . . O Heart, we are old;
> The living beauty is for younger men;
> We cannot pay its tribute of wild tears.

'The Living Beauty'[1] and 'A Song'[2] recorded this realisation of age; but in 'The Wild Swans at Coole',[3] written in the autumn of 1916, his lament for loneliness and lost youth is blended skilfully into the hauntingly evocative description of the swans. This poem was written in a mood of depression; when Yeats had first stayed at Coole in 1897 he was then nervously exhausted. His affair with Diana Vernon had ended; he was 'tortured with sexual desire and disappointed love'; and as he walked in the woods at Coole 'it would have been a relief to have screamed aloud'.

The change between the ages of thirty-two and fifty-one is measured in the sudden realisation that love itself can die. 'For who could have foretold / That the heart grows old?' Here in Coole he had been 'sad and miserable' because Maud would not marry him, and now he is equally sad and miserable because her present refusal to marry him has not caused him deep concern. He is like the solitary poet in *Alastor* who is disturbed by the sight of the swan which rises in flight on its return home to its mate. (There are several other points of similarity between the poems; the preface to *Alastor* sketches the poet as seeking in vain a prototype of his conception of the ideal person he could love; both poems are also concerned with sleep.) Unlike the swans in Coole lake who are unwearied of love, Yeats is 'worn out with dreams', his heart has grown cold, and, in 'Men Improve with the Years',[4] he regrets that youth has been replaced by wisdom.

When Iseult finally refused him in 1917 he married Georgie Hyde

---

[1] *CP*, 156.   [2] *CP*, 156.   [3] *CP*, 147.   [4] *CP*, 152.

Lees, whom he had known for some years. At first he was deeply disturbed, as 'Owen Aherne and His Dancers' makes clear:

The Heart behind its rib laughed out. 'You have called me mad,' it said,
'Because I made you turn away and run from that young child;
How could she mate with fifty years that was so wildly bred?
Let the cage bird and the cage bird mate and the wild bird mate in the
    wild.'
'You but imagine lies all day, O murderer,' I replied.
'And all those lies have but one end, poor wretches to betray;
I did not find in any cage the woman at my side.
O but her heart would break to learn my thoughts are far away.'
'Speak all your mind,' my Heart sang out, 'speak all your mind; who
    cares,
Now that your tongue cannot persuade the child till she mistake
Her childish gratitude for love and match your fifty years?
O let her choose a young man now and all for his wild sake.'[1]

There were other poems to Iseult: 'To a Young Beauty'[2] and 'To a Young Girl',[3] both expressing concern about her immersion in Dublin's bohemian circles; 'Michael Robartes and the Dancer',[4] with its genial emphasis on the need to study and respect her beauty; and 'Two Songs of a Fool',[5] indicating his fear that in the preoccupation of marriage he might have neglected the great feeling of responsibility he had for her, the tame hare. But his cry of 'O Heart, we are old' became lulled in the poems mirroring aspects of his marriage, 'Solomon to Sheba',[6] 'An Image from a Past Life'[7] and 'Solomon and the Witch'.[8] Wisdom and love seemed suddenly to be successfully combined in marriage.

The reason for this was that Mrs. Yeats realised Yeats was very unhappy and thought he needed something to keep him from brooding on personal problems, so being a medium and knowing Yeats's interest in the supernatural, she decided four days after their marriage to attempt automatic writing. Yeats tells us what happened in *A Packet for Ezra Pound*:

What came in disjointed sentences, in almost illegible writing, was so exciting, sometimes so profound, that I persuaded her to give an hour or so day after day to the unknown writers and after some half

[1] CP, 247.   [2] CP, 157.   [3] CP, 157.   [4] CP, 197.
[5] CP, 190.   [6] CP, 155.   [7] CP, 200.   [8] CP, 199.

dozen such hours offered to spend what remained of life explaining and piecing together those scattered sentences. 'No,' was the answer, 'we have come to give you metaphors for poetry.'

Through this writing came the authority Yeats had sought in vain in his early membership of arcane societies. His scepticism was sufficiently lulled like his consciousness of age, for him to find the simplicity he had sought in vain. He need no longer, he said, write poems like 'The Phases of the Moon'[1] and 'Ego Dominus Tuus'[2] (to these poems of *The Wild Swans of Coole* we might add 'The Magi'[3] of *Responsibilities*). He embarked upon the writing of *A Vision*, and this work in addition to providing him with metaphors for poetry gave him a scaffolding for his ideas. Originally he had sought shelter from scepticism and from orthodoxy in secrecy and in the oracular wisdom of others: now he could rely upon his own thought and the ideas of *A Vision* enough to unite triumphantly in his poetry his theoretical idealism of the eighties and nineties, and his attempt to find an Irish literary heritage, with the antithesis to these efforts, the denationalised realism and disillusion of his middle period. His style was now flexible enough to match its rightful subject, himself, the poet Yeats.

There were other reasons, of course, for the great blossoming of his poetry which occurred after his marriage, beside the excitement of the automatic writing and the attempt to piece together ideas it brought or liberated on history and personality. Many of these he had been forming for some time or seizing upon in conversations, or finding in his reading, both in orthodox literature and in the heterodox writings he had been steadily assimilating since his teens. He had left behind a long barren passion for a marriage which meant the continuation of the Yeats line, for the birth of his daughter Anne in 1919 was followed by that of his son Michael Butler in 1921. He was sharing in the common experience of man. He decided to live in the summer months in the Norman tower he had bought in 1915 at Gort near Coole; he was symbolising thus his return to the tradition of the Anglo-Irish, blending Shelleyan dreams of towers as places of wisdom with the simpler pleasure of living in his own house, and that a place of legend in his own country. The Irish Free State had made him a member of its first Senate: this synthesis of the extremes of revolutionary and sceptic was a happy one. He played a more positive role than is normally realised in the Senate; he saw to it

[1] *CP*, 183.   [2] *CP*, 180.   [3] *CP*, 141.

C

now that great art should not be beaten down, and his views were taken seriously. The award of the Nobel prize for poetry in 1923 offset the old Dublin feeling that Yeats was 'finished' when he had published his *Collected Works* in 1908.

He had begun to write his great poetry; he was free to express himself, his hates as well as loves, his sexual lusts as well as romantic memories, and his thoughts, above all, upon death. For, like Donne, he was pre-occupied with death; he kept asking the same questions; he kept the energy and intensity to rediscover ideas and rehandle them with an ever richer stock of symbols, of vocabulary. There are many poems which do not depend directly upon *A Vision*, however much the whole back-ground of the work upon that book created the masterly creative mood out of which they sprang. Perhaps the best of these is 'In Memory of Major Robert Gregory'.[1]

The great quality of this poem is its directness. While not easily con-versational, indeed at times syntactically highly complex, even clumsy (look at stanza IV, for instance), the poet is none the less talking to us. This is a *tour de force*, a public poem which is also private. We are allowed to overhear Yeats thinking aloud, yet retaining his intense privacy. To expose the intensity of personal emotion without vulgarity, to elevate private grief into a general sorrow, is a mark of the major poet, and the first stanza shows us how this is going to be done. The note is quiet, even deceptively casual at first:

> Now that we're almost settled in our house
> I'll name the friends that cannot sup with us
> Beside a fire of turf in th' ancient tower,
> And having talked to some late hour
> Climb up the narrow winding stair to bed:
> Discoverers of forgotten truth
> Or mere companions of my youth,
> All, all are in my thoughts tonight being dead.

The 'almost' is deliberately informal. The house seems at first merely introduced as part of the conversation, yet it is steadily to attain signi-ficance as the poem progresses. Robert Gregory loved it; he was an artist; he could have counselled Yeats in its intricacies. But then it is an unusual house; it is an ancient tower in Ireland, as the tactful description of the fire indicates; it has a narrow winding stair. Its age, its history,

[1] *CP*, 148.

its stair will all become known later in Yeats's poetry, for his symbols had to gain their effect by repetition and modification. The air of mystery given by the fact that the poet is living in an ancient tower is added to by the description of the friends who cannot sup with him as 'Discoverers of forgotten truth'; yet, with good manners, the poet does not maintain this note too long, and adds 'Or mere companions of my youth'. So far, this is a setting of the scene and we are brought into sympathy; we are thinking of the friendships which are cemented in talk in the late hours, talk about truth; and then the friends are companions of the poet's youth. The emotion suddenly tautens with the skilful repetition of 'all', the realisation that all these friends are dead, the emphasis upon their *being* dead. The last line of the stanza is not conversational then, but thematic. We are now prepared for the memories and the comments which will equally rise above conversational tone and yet, because the setting and the tone have been so subtly established, will seem a natural communication of thought. The transition from setting to speech, and them, in stanza VI, from speech to subject is masterly:

> They were my close companions many a year,
> A portion of my mind and life, as it were,
> And now their breathless faces seem to look
> Out of some old picture book;
> I am accustomed to their lack of breath,
> But not that my dear friend's dear son,
> Our Sidney and our perfect man,
> Could share in that discourtesy of death.

The Elizabethan parallel to Sidney whose love of action led him to his soldier's death abroad is suggested delicately. It prepares us for the later praise of Gregory's unusual versatility. Yeats uses repetition skilfully here, the echo of '*dear* friend's *dear* son' caught up again in '*Our* Sidney and *our* perfect man'. This serves as an introduction to the later repetition of 'Soldier, scholar, horseman, he'. Stanzas IX, X and XI are the kernel of the poem, and their praise of Gregory avoids fulsomeness by being elevated into a kind of ritual in which this line provides a constant element. Then there comes the quiet return to the simplicity with which the poem began, and to the end of what has been revealed of the poet's feelings:

> . . . a thought
> Of that late death took all my heart for speech.

To Yeats Gregory had been a supreme example of self-confidence. There are many pages about him in Yeats's 1910 Diary, even a letter that was never sent. Yeats envied Gregory his lack of introspection, and it is probably because of this that he was to write in 'An Irish Airman Foresees his Death'[1] perhaps the most perceptive of all poems about the mystique of flying with its concentration upon the essential issue in two lines:

> A lonely impulse of delight
> Drove to this tumult in the clouds.

8. *Michael Robartes and the Dancer*

In examining the first poems which arise out of Yeats's preoccupation with the 'system' of thought expounded in the two editions of *A Vision* it may be useful to comment at the same time upon the 'metaphors for poetry' which it provides.

A Vision enabled Yeats 'to hold in a single thought reality and justice'; in answer to an imagined query as to whether he believed in the existence of the circuits of the sun and moon in *A Vision*, he called them 'stylistic arrangements of experience'. The book provides a scaffolding for his erection of an increasingly personal mythology, a task attempted by many twentieth-century poets, hankering after, as Robert Graves called it, the 'Christian myth cycle' as a 'secure basis of poetic reference', yet writing in an age when they think it hard to accept the validity of Christian or of Classical images or ideas.[2]

There are two main elements in *A Vision*. One is an attempt to categorise human beings, to see in them abstract qualities and to make them mythological figures in the process. This is symbolised by the phases of the moon, which give twenty-eight categories. The diagram in *A Vision* shows how the sun equals objectivity, the moon subjectivity, and how subjectivity increases until in phase eight there is an equal amount of subjectivity and objectivity. Subjectivity predominates from the eighth phase until the twenty-second, where objectivity increases. Phases eight to twenty-two (predominantly objective) are *primary*, whereas phases nine to twenty-one (primarily subjective) are *antithetical*. The system is one of conflict, where men of the first fourteen phases seek their opposite

---

[1] *CP*, 152.   [2] J. M. Cohen, *Robert Graves*, 1960, p. 90.

(their 'mask', their object of will) from among phases sixteen to twenty-seven and vice versa.

This Blake-like doctrine—Yeats liked quoting 'without contraries there is no progression' which he thought 'fundamental in Blake'—probably stems from Yeats's own experience, for he evolved the doctrine of the mask for himself in those difficult years of disillusionment. He had created his character Michael Robartes when he was ill and disappointed in love. Robartes is tough, a successful lover and man of action. Yeats began to see the advantage of imposing an exterior pattern upon an inner being, and later wrote in his Diary that 'all happiness depends upon having the energy to assume the mask of some other self; that all joyous or creative life is a rebirth as something not oneself—something created in a moment and perpetually renewed; in playing a game like that of a child where one loses the infinite pain of self-realisation, a grotesque or solemn painted face put on that one may haste from the terrors of judgment'. This kind of solution was attempted in 'The Grey Rock', but in a very elementary escapist way. The earliest exposition of the tension comes in 'Ego Dominus Tuus' (written in 1915), where *Hic* and *Ille* represent objective and subjective elements. The poem is an elaboration of the search for an opposite (and can be glossed by *Per Amica Silentia Lunae*, a prose work of 1917), and *Ille*'s call to his own opposite, 'the image' or anti-self, is gradually explained.

The poem anticipates the structure of later poems; its apparent conclusion is at the beginning, its meaning only to be fully realised after the condensed explanation or parallel in the middle of the poem. Yeats's technique of reworking and rewriting often meant that the poem departed far from its original draft. The poem centres upon Dante, in whom Yeats (perhaps wiser than Rossetti) detected an inner conflict. Dante was placed in the seventeenth phase of *A Vision*; his true mask was the pursuit of simplification through intensity, his false one 'dispersal'. This is the phase in which Unity of Being is sought. And unity was one of the objects of Yeats's own searching; he thought of himself as a man of this phase. But when he wrote this poem in 1915 he had not yet been able to achieve the necessary confidence to use himself as the sole battleground for the antithetical struggle.

This is one of the differences between 'Ego Dominus Tuus'[1] and 'The Phases of the Moon'.[2] In the latter poem the antithetical *persona* has moved away from mere tracing of magical shapes; he is now nearly

[1] *CP*, 180.   [2] *CP*, 183.

Yeats himself in his tower; but not completely. Robartes and Aherne,
his imaginary characters, replace *Hic* and *Ille*; but they add a third
dimension by describing Yeats who has

> chosen this place to live in
> Because, it may be, of the candle-light
> From the far tower where Milton's Platonist
> Sat late, or Shelley's visionary prince:
> The lonely light that Samuel Palmer engraved,
> For image of mysterious wisdom won by toil;
> And now he seeks in book and manuscript
> What he shall never find.

The Yeats here described has moved away from the dubious reception of
wisdom that has replaced youth. Now he is to present himself as a poet
of power and affirmation, a man of learning; he is returning to one of
the two mythological images which Shelley used, of the young man
whose hair has grown white from the burden of his thoughts and 'an
old man in some shell-strewn cave whom it is possible to call, when
speaking to the Sultan, "as inaccessible as God or thou"'.[1]

'The Phases of the Moon' describes the material of *A Vision*, but it is
too close to exposition; it required the prose glossing which can be provided, and without it is not sufficiently charged to live its own life as a
poem. 'The Double Vision of Michael Robartes'[2] is very different.
Here Yeats infuses his symbolism with imagination; he is condensing
and, by being particular and precise, contriving to convey an unworldly
weirdly dreaming effect.

This poem owes some of its strength to the other main element in *A
Vision*, Yeats's view of history. He saw history as a series of cyclical
processes, as had many before him: Empedocles, Heracleitus, Plato,
Swedenborg, Boehme and Blake, to name a few whom he had studied.
He had many points of departure for his ideas; Madame Blavatsky's
teaching; Flinders Petrie's ideas; even the descriptions of an old Irish
countrywoman. He saw time made up of opposing cycles lasting 2,000
years, and he used the diagrams of opposing gyres to illustrate them, a
gyre being the spiral path traced out on a cone. Each age was seen as the
reversal of the previous age; and 'The Double Vision of Michael
Robartes' begins with images of the making of a new cycle of violence,
an idea to be further explored. ('The Magi'[3] with its 'uncontrollable

[1] W. B. Yeats, *A Vision*, 1937, 143.   [2] *CP*, 192.   [3] *CP*, 141.

mystery on the bestial floor' was the first poetic hint of his view that the coming of Christianity ended a period of subjectivity and brought in a civilisation that would last until some new gyre brought in its opposite.)

That is the setting. There follows in the second section a description of the fifteenth phase, which draws upon the past poetry describing Iseult Gonne, and uses it to give reality to abstraction, a thing continued in the third section, which builds the Helen symbolism into the new structure with superb confidence. This confidence is pinpointed in 'Demon and Beast',[1] one of the poems in *Michael Robartes and the Dancer* (1921), which deals in the ideas of *A Vision*, with an ironic use of the images of perning and gyring. But the apogee of Yeats's interest in historical change is 'The Second Coming'.[2] This poem conveys the terror of a coming antithetical civilisation. It creates its effect by its images, by disgust at prevalent anarchy, by horror at the overcoming of innocence, and by its slow, remorseless revelation of the nature of what is to come: the image, gradually glimpsed, is finally appreciated for all its brutality; it is slouching towards Bethlehem, the traditional holy place of Christian worship, to be born. The tension of the poem is continuous; its own movements of repetition and of echo add to the feeling of inevitability which Yeats wants to create. The effect of his new symbols is already beginning to be cumulative. 'Calvary's turbulence' of 'The Magi' is now to be seen in the light of 'The Second Coming's' twenty centuries of stony sleep which were rocked to nightmare by Calvary's rocking cradle. This poem can be laden with annotations giving possible sources, fuller explanations and explications: but its shockwave travels consistently through subsequent readings whether or not these are enriched by the labours of commentators.

'The Second Coming' is a poem the meaning of which depends entirely upon Yeats's private language, and yet, as poem, is independent of his ideas, of his theory of history, his imagery of the gyres, his use of memories of pictures. One of the reasons for its success may be that in it Yeats is alternating his approach. The opening lines are a great evocation of visual response, the force of the 'ing' ending strengthening the idea of continuous movement, which is basic in the poem. The deliberate repetition of 'turning and turning' is half-echoed by the 'falcon', 'falconer' repetition. Then the image is expanded and generalised, centrifugal force is generated with 'Things fall apart; the centre cannot hold'. Tension develops with the effort of the centre, while the image

[1] *CP*, 209.   [2] *CP*, 210.

(and the role) of the falconer is clarified, and the poem extends its subject to the world. The idea of force is suddenly rammed home, and at the same time despised when 'mere anarchy is loosed upon the world'. We realise that the falconer has exerted rule or authority over the falcon: but now the images change; 'loosed' implies the gathering force of anarchy; the word is repeated and intensified with the image of the flooding tide, and the adjective 'blood-dimmed' strengthens the sinister situation, and even may suggest the archetypal myth of floods destroying all life upon the world. The effect is measured in the 'drowning' of innocence. The images return to man, the movement is from the falcon's widening gyration to the sharper final disruption, the failure of the centre, and then the irruption of anarchy is measured against man's decline. The lack of conviction in the best catches up the idea that the centre cannot hold; the passionate intensity of the worst is implicitly linked with the drowning of innocence in the blood-dimmed tide.

These eight brilliantly compressed lines create a terrifying picture of the world's situation. This is complete enough for Yeats to break off and gather his audience with him to assess the meaning of this disruption, this cataclysmic process. The idea of the second coming is the only possible response big enough for such a predicament, and with the idea comes the image. Here Yeats changes his approach and allows the sound of the poem to be largely dominated by the beat of single syllables, while the force shifts slowly from the concrete nouns which affect our visual power (sands, desert, shape, lion, body, head, man, gaze, thighs, shadows, desert birds) through the guidance of adjectives ('blank and pitiless', to stress the brutality, 'slow' thighs for horror and inexorability, and even the birds are 'indignant') to the abstract words which carry the poem's extensions. Darkness, stony sleep, nightmare and the rocking cradle (of Christ) all demand our imagination's rapid and lively response; they are all symbols, their suggestiveness is taut with expectancy. It is time to ask the question—to turn the 'vast image', already suggested grimly enough in 'lion body and the head of a man', into an even more terrifying abstraction of 'what rough beast'—an image which gains its full ghastliness because of the deliberate inevitability of 'its hour come round at last' (where the 'its' still carries the memory of 'its slow thighs') and because, with our realisation that this heralds the end of the ceremony of innocence, the end of the Christian dispensation, the desecration of the Holy Place of Bethlehem, comes the ultimate horror carried by the steadily culminating intensification of the meaning of the verbs—'reel', 'vexed' and, finally, the keyword which carries with it the whole weight of the poem's strength, 'slouches'. This is probably Yeats's most powerful poem; its effect is cumulative; it states a situation and envisages its development, its essence is dramatic as well as philosophic, lyric as well as elegaic.

In 'A Prayer for my Daughter' this coming of ruin upon civilisation preoccupies Yeats:

> Imagining in excited reverie
> That the future years had come,
> Dancing to a frenzied drum,
> Out of the murderous innocence of the sea.[1]

But this poem shows the flexibility he was achieving. It can move through description of the place we are beginning to recognise, the tower; it can freely describe the poet's mood of gloom and then move to the idea of beauty in women, from there to symbols of great love found disappointing, to Helen, Aphrodite and by implication Maud Gonne. There is a praise of courtesy, charm, wisdom and the glad kindness (that Yeats had found in marriage) as well as a hope for merriment. Then comes the terrible denunciation of intellectual hatred and of Maud Gonne, the loveliest woman born, whose opinionated mind is savagely attacked. The last stanzas praise innocence, and custom and ceremony. This poem is an amalgam of symbols, its richness of texture is remarkable, and its easy flow of ideas, more subtly linked than may at first appear, is a result of Yeats's increasing ability to make his concepts cohere. This is a compound of love and hatred; the scorn for the thoroughfares reminds us of the little streets Maud Gonne would have thrown upon the great ('No Second Troy');[2] the praise of innocence and beauty goes back to idealistic youthfulness when merriment was possible ('The Fiddler of Dooney').[3] It is, however, self-knowing:

> My mind, because the minds that I have loved,
> The sort of beauty that I have approved,
> Prosper but little, has dried up of late,
> Yet knows that to be choked with hate
> May well be of all evil chances chief.

[1] CP, 211.   [2] CP, 101.   [3] CP, 82.

9. *The Tower*

Complex and vigorous poetry continues in *The Tower*, which contains Yeats's richest texture of poetry: 'Sailing to Byzantium',[1] 'The Tower',[2] 'Meditations in Time of Civil War',[3] 'Nineteen Hundred and Nineteen',[4] 'Leda and the Swan',[5] 'Among School Children'[6] and 'All Souls' Night'.[7] Yeats had devoted his life to poetry in the Celtic twilight period (like a white-haired Shelleyan young man, he told Katharine Tynan when he was twenty-four that he had brayed his life in a mortar), but now life had become so exciting that poetry must be devoted to it. As a result, there are contradictions. They were an essential part of Yeats's being. He can praise Plato and Plotinus in lieu of the Muse in the first section of 'The Tower', then veer to the opposite extreme and

> . . . mock Plotinus' thought
> And cry in Plato's teeth,
> Death and life were not
> Till man made up the whole,
> Made lock, stock and barrel
> Out of his bitter soul . . .

This is part and parcel of his own problem. He was torn between passionate regret for the waning of physical strength and desire to 'make his soul' with things of the mind and spirit.

Naturally this kind of conflict does not continue in cut and dried terms, though an occasional poem may provide its specific but temporary answer. 'Sailing to Byzantium', for instance, began as an expression of dislike of his own age. The original drafts illustrate this: the first stanza ran:

> All in this land—my Maker that is play
> Or else asleep upon His Mother's knees,
> Others, that as the mountain people say
> Are at their hunting and their gallantries
> Under the hills as in our fathers' day
> The changing colours of the hills and seas

[1] *CP*, 217. [2] *CP*, 218. [3] *CP*, 225. [4] *CP*, 232
[5] *CP*, 241. [6] *CP*, 242. [7] *CP*, 256.

> All that men know or think they know, being young,
> Cry that my tale is told, my story sung.

This was followed by a version which began more directly 'Here all is young', and this is the reason for the poet's wish to leave the sensuous life of Ireland as the draft of the second stanza indicated, 'I therefore travel towards Byzantium'. By the time the poem was in its final form the poet had to be more interested in Byzantium than in Ireland, and had begun to look back at Ireland from the vantage point achieved in the poem, so that the opening line of the poem 'That is no country for old men' refers to Ireland.

The natural images of the first stanza present youthful vigour, the second an image of age (related to that of 'Among School Children'[1]) from which comes the transition, in the third, from the 'dying animal' to the 'artifice of eternity'. Here we have a characteristic piece of honesty. Yeats is careful to match 'eternity' with 'artifice', indulging not merely in metaphysical paradox, but being true to his own blend of assertion and doubt. The fourth stanza with its artificial bird is an image of supernatural wisdom: its sources are legion. It may come from the Order of the Golden Dawn, it may come from elsewhere in Yeats's reading, perhaps as Ernest Schanzer suggests from a childhood memory of Hans Andersen's 'The Emperor's Nightingale'.[2] It is detached from the flux of human life, from what is past or passing or to come. Only 'out of nature' can any escape from the tyranny of time be envisaged. And Byzantium is chosen because of the historical role Yeats saw for it in *A Vision* the saints are to 'perne in a gyre' because of their part in that role:

> in early Byzantium, and maybe never before or since in recorded history, religious, aesthetic, and practical life were one, and . . . architect and artificer—though not, it may be, poets, for language had been the instrument of controversy and must have grown abstract—spoke to the multitude and the few alike. The painter and the mosaic worker, the worker in gold and silver, the illuminator of sacred books were almost impersonal, almost perhaps without the consciousness of individual design absorbed in their subject matter and that the vision of a whole people.

Yeats is blending here his visual memories of mosaics at Ravenna, and his reading about Byzantium in such scholarly works as W. G. Holmes's

---

[1] *CP*, 242. [2] Ernest Schanzer, *English Studies*, XLI, 6, Dec. 1960.

The Age of Justinian and Theodora, O. M. Dalton's *Byzantine Art and Archaeology*, Mrs. Strong's *Apostheosis and After Life* and Gibbon's *Decline and Fall*.

Other poems return to the idea of the historical gyres. The sonnet 'Leda and the Swan',[1] closely related to Michelangelo's painting in Venice,[2] is another metaphorical treatment of the moment of annunciation, prompted by Yeats's feeling that some starting-point for a new cycle was imminent in his own period. He sees Grecian civilisation beginning with the myth of Leda, 'remembering that they showed in a Spartan temple strung up to the roof as a holy relic, an unhatched egg of hers, and that from one of her eggs came love and from the other war'. The symbol of Leda is enriched by the previous poems which focused upon Helen and the ruin of Troy, and we are thus prepared for—

> The broken wall, the burning roof and tower
> And Agamemnon dead.

The swan is again to be used as a symbol of power, even of war, and the problem posed here is whether opposites ever coincide, whether the antimonies must be forever opposed—a suggestion made in 'Solomon and the Witch'[3] that Chance and Choice were for once united, and—

> He that crowed out eternity
> Thought to have crowed it in again.

This same metaphor of annunciation gives 'Two Songs from a Play'[4] great dramatic strength. These songs are extremely condensed and operate at several levels of mythology. The basic idea is that the coming of Christianity terminated the 2,000-year cycle of history which preceded it and ushered in its own era with radical violence. The myth of Dionysus is used for parallel and Athena the 'staring' trance-like virgin is so described to give an air of cyclic inevitability to the occurrence of the death of Dionysus (the child of mortal Persephone and immortal Zeus) at the hands of the Titans. 'Magnus Annus' suggests that the death and rebirth of the god occurs as part of the recurring cycles of history. The image of the 'beating heart' comes from Yeats's reading in Sir William Crookes, *Studies in Psychical Resarch*, and he is also thinking (as he had earlier in *The Tables of the Law* and *The Adoration of the Magi*)

---

[1] *CP*, 241.
[2] See Giorgio Melchiori, *The Whole Mystery of Art*, 1960, p. 153.
[3] *CP*, 199.   [4] *CP*, 239.

of Vigil's famous prophecy in *Eclogue IV*, where Virgo, daughter of Jupiter and Themis, is to return to earth bringing the golden age. This was sometimes read, particularly in the Middle Ages, as foretelling the coming of Mary and Christ (as the Star of Bethlehem). Shelley's *Hellas* provides imagery for the return of the Argo (though Yeats does not echo his optimism) as does William Morris's *The Life and Death of Jason*.

The second song catches up the idea of 'The Magi',[1] and is linked to 'Wisdom',[2] and we realise that 'The Second Coming' is itself seen as an equally disruptive repetition of the earlier Christian annunciation, itself an echo of the earlier classical theophanies. The 'fabulous formless darkness' derives from Proclus, whom Yeats read in translation, and the Babylonian astrologers probably reduce by their divination man's significance in the total scheme and history of the universe. The brevity of his existence is intensified in the self-burning consuming fire of his creative moments. Here is the paradox again: unity of being was to be sought but cannot endure. This is the thought of 'In Memory of Major Robert Gregory'[3] crystallised in a new way:

> The bare chimney is gone black out
> Because the work had finished in that flare.

'The Tower'[4] is a companion piece to 'Sailing to Byzantium',[5] for it states the problem of old age and revolves round the image of the fisherman which Yeats had earlier used to portray his ideal man. In the first section of this poem he refers to his own fishing on Ben Bulben as a boy, saying he now has a more 'Excited passionate fantastical' imagination than then, and yet must because of old age subdue it into interest in abstract things. The second section is a *tour de force* of this passionate imagination. Images and memories are blended, as are the aristocratic Mrs. French (the subject of an eighteenth-century anecdote related by Sir Jonah Barrington in his *Recollections*) and the peasant girl Mary Hynes (this story, and blind Raftery's poem about her are included in Yeats's *The Celtic Twilight*). The movement from Raftery to Homer, from Helen to Maud Gonne is subtle and economical. Then there comes the recollection of Yeats's invention of Red Hanrahan, and then the poet turns to the Tower's inhabitants. All of them are summoned to his query: did they rage as he does against old age? And the poem,

[1] *CP*, 141.   [2] *CP*, 246.   [3] *CP*, 148.
[4] *CP*, 218.   [5] *CP*, 217.

through Hanrahan the lover, turns to a great penetrating and searing honesty about love:

> Does the imagination dwell the most
> Upon a woman won or woman lost?
> If on the lost, admit you turned aside
> From a great labyrinth out of pride,
> Cowardice, some silly over-subtle thought
> Or anything called conscience once;
> And that if memory recur, the sun's
> Under eclipse and the day blotted out.

The last section winds its way through a praise of young men in the Anglo-Irish tradition of Burke and Grattan 'That gave, though free to refuse', and a praise of man's 'bitter soul', before returning to the young men to remark that the poet was once of their sort—a remark which links the poem together, referring back as it does to his own youthful fishing on Ben Bulben. Finally, he catches up love's memory and its passionate blotting out of the day by using a ninety-ish twilight cadence, reinforced not by a Miltonic 'all passion spent' but by a soul he has been compelled to study while the body's decay and worse—

> Seem but the clouds of the sky
> When the horizon fades;
> Or a bird's sleepy cry
> Among the deepening shades.

The Irish civil war was for Yeats a microcosm in which he could study violence and hatred. It affected him as the 1914–1918 War had not; it extended the feelings engendered in him by the 1916 Rebellion. In 'Meditations in Time of Civil War'[1] he records his conversations with Irregulars and Government troops and returns to lonely contemplation. The observation of the moor-hen is casually done, yet masterly:

> I count those feathered balls of soot
> The moor-hen guides upon the stream,
> To silence the envy in my thought;
> And turn towards my chamber, caught
> In the cold snows of a dream.

It is casual, because his envy of men of action, the very act of contemplation itself, is bitter and swamps the pleasure:

[1] CP, 225.

We had fed the heart on fantasies,
The heart's grown brutal from the fare;
More substance in our enmities
Than in our love; O honey-bees,
Come build in the empty house of the stare.

The bees (apart from their possible derivation from mystic tradition in Porphyry) may symbolise patience and creative force as opposed to destructive forces at work in Ireland. He is preoccupied with the loss of gentleness and sweetness, for killing and the destruction of great houses goes on around him:

We are closed in and the key is turned
On our uncertainty; somewhere
A man is killed, or a house burned,
Yet no clear fact to be discerned:
Come build in the empty house of the stare.

Yet he realises that even the great houses of the rich were probably erected by violent, bitter, powerful men. He argues that the image for the inherited glory of the rich—despite the fact that we might expect to find life in their demesnes overflowing 'without ambitious pains'—should be an empty sea-shell (an image derived from Shelley). This is because when the violence or bitterness which existed in the founders of these houses goes from their descendants greatness also may vanish. The problem posed in the first section develops more personally in the second, where he describes his tower home, skilfully bridging the idea that violence created the great houses of the rich by telling us how a man-at-arms had founded his own tower—

In this tumultuous spot,
Where through long wars and sudden night alarms
His dwindling score and he seemed castaways
Forgetting and forgot.

Yeats had followed him—

that after me
My bodily heirs may find,
To exalt a lonely mind,
Befitting emblems of adversity.

The image of a lasting art, of its transmission through families, through centuries, follows in the description of Sato's sword in the third section, the whole caught up in the question put in the next section of how the poet's children will fare in life, in the human situation where the inherited flower of life lasts but a brief spell of time. The poem moves through the problem of the tower's possible fate (the bridge leading to it was blown up by Republican forces) to the civil war images of the fifth and sixth sections and finally to the vision in the last section of hatred and its effect on men. The poet himself must be content in days of violence with abstract joy and 'The half-read wisdoms of daemonic images'.

In part the sections of this poem are linked by the poet's personality, in part by his sense of history. This architectonic quality emerges in 'Nineteen Hundred and Nineteen'[1] as well, a poem which shapes itself out of Yeats's thoughts upon the change created by the violence which followed the 1916 rising, the Black and Tans (the 'drunken soldiery' of the fourth stanza), the ambushes, the burnings of houses. The attitude Yeats adopts to all this is at once stoical and romantic:

> But is there any comfort to be found?
> Man is in love, and loves what vanishes,
> What more is there to say?

The stoicism derives from *A Vision*'s ideas upon the remorseless process of historical change; the romantic quality is subtly achieved by reference to the heroic symbols of Athens:

> That country round
> None dared admit, if such a thought were his,
> Incendiary or bigot could be found
> To burn that stump on the Acropolis.
> Or break in bits the famous ivories
> Or traffic in the grasshoppers or bees.

The image of a heroic Athens at war continues through the reference to the Platonic year (a part of his thinking in *A Vision*, now whirled in by the dancers and their dragon of air, which reminds us that days in Ireland are now 'dragon-ridden'; the idea extends from these Chinese dancers to the dance which men perform in life) which 'Whirls out new right and wrong, / Whirls in the old instead' and leads to the 'Platonist's' affirmation whereby Yeats comes to measure the futility of having dreamed of mending the mischief of mankind. The swan symbol carries

[1] *CP*, 232.

several meanings; it brought the beginning of the Grecian cycle; it was a symbol of war; and here it also symbolises the solitary soul, as later in 'Coole Park and Ballylee, 1931'[1] it symbolised inspiration. Though the image of the weasel and the heartfelt echo of Blake's lines on mockery (and the Irish poet James Clarence Mangan's fine poem 'Gone in the Wind') the poem concludes with its tumult of images, of violence culminating in the horror of the witch and her demon.

Even a change from the uncertainties of Ballylee to the slumbrous air of pre-industrial Oxford in 1920 could not lull Yeats's restless preoccupation with the stylisation of his experience into patterns of thought which included the gyring movement of historical change. 'All Souls' Night',[2] its atmospheric quality superbly evoked (it was written in a moment of exaltation),[3] turns upon the twisting of 'mummy cloth' (a symbol of the winding of time, of life, of history as in 'His Bargain'). Its personae, Horton, Florence Emery and MacGregor Mathers (all seekers after hidden truth who believed it would be revealed to them) are subordinate to the poet's ponderings upon thoughts of the soul's journey and images of the dance.

'Among School Children'[4] uses the dance image with great effect. In this poem Yeats displays consummate ability in keeping his complex, widely-ranging thought linked to the setting of the poem. The description of the schoolroom derives from the interest he formed in education when he was a Senator, visiting schools, talking to school-teachers and making sensible suggestions in speeches. The tone is deprecating: the sixty-year-old smiling public man's views of education were probably far from those informing 'the best modern way' of the nuns. But behind this benign mask lurked memories of Maud Gonne and her recollections of her childhood. The poet looks at the children and wonders—

> if she stood so at that age—
> For even daughters of the swan can share
> Something of every paddler's heritage—
> And had that colour upon cheek or hair,
> And thereupon my heart is driven wild:
> She stands before me as a living child.

To allow this intensity to develop so early in the poem, and then to guide it into 'Her present image' and from that into the poet's youth

[1] CP, 275.   [2] CP, 256.
[3] W. B. Yeats, A Vision, 1925, p. xii. [4] CP, 242.

D

and present appearance, 'a comfortable kind of old scarecrow', is masterly. The particular moves into the general with echoes of Donne and of peasant speech in the fifth stanza, where the problem of age is put sharply in the contrast between the youthful mother with her child and the sixty-year-old man her child becomes. The use of Porphyry's image—'honey of generation'—leads to a comment in the next stanza upon the inability of three wise men, Plato, Aristotle and Pythagoras, to rise by thought above the common condition: they are (like the old man in 'Sailing to Byzantium', like the public man in this poem), 'old clothes upon old sticks to scare a bird' by the time their fame has come.

Yet there are images which survive the questioning of life, of time, the nuns' images, the mothers' images; these can also be the images of art, that 'keep a marble or a bronze repose'. These images can, however, seem to the poet 'mere images' in contrast to real live beauty; he needs to elevate them further, or they will never satisfy—and hence the image of the dancer in 'Among School Children', which is 'self born', out of mortality, created by the imagination, as is the image of the tree (here standing for the beauty of life itself). These images are created by an isolated poet, and this poem is in part recording the cost, the tragic irony of the poet's conception of a state of perfection outside life, of being rather than becoming, out of nature into the timeless changelessness of art, this state accentuated by and accentuating the tragedy of our being born but to die, our being, paradoxically, dying generations.

10. *The Winding Stair and Words for Music Perhaps*

This value of the image or the artifact comes out strongly in 'Byzantium',[1] where Yeats is not so much concerned with 'Sailing to Byzantium's' 'dying generations', its 'young in one another's arms' and its immense natural vigour as with the state arrived at by the creative imagination, the stillness at the core of the flame-begotten spirits. This poem itself—

[1] CP, 280.

disdains
All that man is,
All mere complexities
The fury and the mire of human veins.

Its bird is meant to carry the idea of 'Sailing to Byzantium' further; it can 'scorn aloud' the living bird; it may even have reached the top of the mystic 'tree of life'.[1] This is a poem rejecting the 'unpurged images' of the natural world, the soldiers and the night-walkers; in it the soul is purified in fire and may retrace the path of life symbolised by 'Hades' bobbin bound in mummy cloth', an idea foreshadowed in 'All Souls' Night'.[2]

   This poem is of richer texture than 'Sailing to Byzantium', and the interlocking of its structure is remarkable. The developing meanings of 'images', 'complexities', 'spirit' and 'fury', for instance, repay very careful, close reading. The echo of the apparently paradoxical lines 'A mouth that has no moisture and no breath / Breathless mouths may summon' in 'Flames that no faggot feeds, nor steel has lit' is part of the technique for achieving cohesiveness. The comparatives emphasise the climactic authority: 'Shade more than man, more image than a shade' is caught up again in 'Miracle, bird or golden handiwork / More miracle than bird or handiwork'. This is the best kind of rhetoric at work; it reinforces the poet's imaginative concept with detail both evocative and authoritative, and it holds together, through its use of symbols, an immense amount of diverse meaning which can operate at different levels. Its repetition, its almost incantatory repetition, and the interrelationship and building up of its images give it cumulative tension. Though this poem is about the soul and its purification, we are not allowed to forget 'The fury and the mire of human veins', out of which the spirits may escape: the complexities may leave in the penultimate stanza; but all the time the process continues, as the last stanza reminds us, as the 'mire and blood' of the dolphins thresh through the sea of life with their cargo of the dead.

   'Byzantium' was written in 1930, four years after 'Sailing to Byzantium'. But within these four years Yeats did not simply strengthen his position within the realm of intellective as opposed to instinctive life. The confidence within which he wrote in the twenties continued beyond

[1] F. A. C. Wilson, *Yeats's Iconography*, 1960, p. 263.
[2] *CP*, 256.

the early *Hic* and *Ille* division; beyond blowing hot and cold on Plato and Plotinus in 'The Tower' it developed into fine metaphysical poems in *The Winding Stair*, such as 'A Dialogue of Self and Soul'.[1] His soul summons him to climb the ancient winding stair, to pursue wisdom, and asks:

> Why should the imagination of a man
> Long past his prime remember things that are
> Emblematic of love and war?
> Think of ancestral night that can,
> If but imagination scorn the earth
> And intellect its wandering
> To this and that and t'other thing,
> Deliver from the crime of death and birth.

The final answer of his self to this is the triumphant assertion of the worth of life:

> I am content to follow to its source
> Every event in action or in thought;
> Measure the lot; forgive myself the lot!
> When such as I cast out remorse
> So great a sweetness flows into the breast
> We must laugh and we must sing,
> We are blest by everything,
> Everything we look upon is blest.

This is an acceptance of life (or perhaps if we note the phrase 'What matter if the ditches are impure?' of death) which is opposed to his Byzantine goals. There should be no difficulty here; the contradiction is implicit in Yeats's thought and is put in 'The Choice':

> The intellect of man is forced to choose
> Perfection of the life or of the work,
> And if it take the second must refuse
> A heavenly mansion, raging in the dark.[2]

Many critics have said this is a false choice; but Yeats drew his anti-thetical tensions from this deliberate alternation. The virtue of the position he had attained was that he could take sides and not worry so much about unity the unity was in his containing extremes within

---

[1] *CP*, 265.   [2] *CP*, 278.

himself and using them as material for poetry. 'Vacillation' expresses this inner conflict:

> Between extremities
> Man runs his course;
> A brand, or flaming breath,
> Comes to destroy
> All those antinomies
> Of day and night;
> The body calls it death,
> The heart remorse.
> But if these be right
> What is joy?[1]

The image of the tree in the second section is an image of joyous life and the fourth section (glossed in *Essays*) describes a state of happiness, but after *The Soul* has advised in Section VII the kind of purification involved in 'Byzantium', 'Look on that fire, salvation walks within', *The Heart* replies with: 'What theme had Homer but original sin?' This is the final answer, a rejection of Von Hugel's Christianity in favour of Homer's 'unchristened heart'.

But these poems in *The Winding Stair* are only part of its variety. There are three poems, 'In Memory of Eva Gore-Booth and Con Markiewicz',[2] 'Coole Park, 1929'[3] and 'Coole Park and Ballylee, 1931',[4] in which Yeats draws upon memories, mingles personal symbolism with them so that a casual reader may be unaware of the symbolic overtones, and creates in the process a Homeric simplicity which conveys his regard and his respect for his friends. (More personal memories appear in 'Quarrel in Old Age',[5] 'The Results of Thought'[6] and 'Stream and Sun at Glendalough';[7] less obvious, though none the less emotionally felt, are the connections between the assassination of the Irish statesman Kevin O'Higgins and 'Death'[8] and 'Blood and the Moon'.)[9] The poems about Coole have a largeness of vision going beyond their grand manner. 'Coole Park and Ballylee, 1931'[10] is more successful in its elevation of Lady Gregory's achievement and his own into literary history; the technique is superb; the mystery of life is kept before us as we recognise the place (we remember all the poems describing the scene), the poetic legends that cling to it (Raftery and Mary Hynes in 'The

---

[1] *CP*, 282.   [2] *CP*, 263.   [3] *CP*, 273.   [4] *CP*, 275.   [5] *CP*, 286.
[6] *CP*, 286.   [7] *CP*, 288.   [8] *CP*, 264.   [9] *CP*, 267.   [10] *CP*, 275.

Tower'), the sheer beauty of Coole, the memories of his own experiences there (suggestions of 'The Wild Swans at Coole'), the swan with
all its symbolic suggestiveness, and then the loving recollection of Coole's
continuity of tradition, of service, of Lady Gregory herself, the last inheritor ('In Memory of Major Robert Gregory'), the great houses
('Nineteen Hundred and Nineteen' and 'Meditations in Time of Civil
War'). Then comes the last stanza pulling together the beauty, the
tradition, Ireland, and the achievement: the end of all the glory, the un-
written question, and the final sinister line:

> We were the last romantics—chose for theme
> Traditional sanctity and loveliness;
> Whatever's written in what poets name
> The book of the people; whatever most can bless
> The mind of man or elevate a rhyme;
> But all is changed, that high horse riderless,
> Though mounted in that saddle Homer rode
> Where the swan drifts upon a darkening flood.

Yeats returned to his Anglo-Irish intellectual inheritance during the
twenties: he developed an affection for Berkeley, whom he began to
read in 1923; and he placed his thought against the mechanical system of
Locke. From Berkeley Yeats went to Wyndham Lewis, Bergson, Croce,
Plato, Plotinus ('The Delphic Oracle upon Plotinus'[1] is almost a translation of Porphyry's Life of Plotinus), and Bertrand Russell. Traces of
this reading appear in such poems as 'Statistics',[2] 'Veronica's Napkin',[3]
'His Bargain'[4] and 'Fragments'.[5] But his interest in Berkeley as an
Anglo-Irish writer was accompanied by an interest in Goldsmith, Burke
and Swift ('Swift's Epitaph'[6] is a brilliant version of the Latin), which
emerges in the second section of 'Blood and the Moon' with its vigorous
vignettes of these men whose inheritor he proclaimed himself to be:

I declare this tower is my symbol; I declare
This winding, gyring, spiring treadmill of a stair is my ancestral stair;
That Goldsmith and the Dean, Berkeley and Burke have travelled there.

Swift beating on his breast in sibylline frenzy blind
Because the heart in his blood-sodden breast had dragged him down into
    mankind,
Goldsmith deliberately sipping at the honey-pot of his mind,

[1] CP, 306.   [2] CP, 271.   [3] CP, 270.
[4] CP, 299.   [5] CP, 240.   [6] CP, 277.

And haughtier-headed Burke that proved the State a tree,
That this unconquerable labyrinth of the birds, century after century,
Cast but dead leaves to mathematical equality;

And God-appointed Berkeley that proved all things a dream,
That this pragmatical, preposterous pig of a world, its farrow that so
  solid seem,
Must vanish on the instant if the mind but change its theme;

Saeva Indignatio and the labourer's hire,
The strength that gives our blood and state magnanimity of its own
  desire;
Everything that is not God consumed with intellectual fire.[1]

In 'The Seven Sages' he sees in them what he himself is now achieving,
an echo of vigorous Irish speech:

> Born in such community Berkeley with his belief in perception,
> that abstract ideas are mere words, Swift with his love of perfect
> nature, of the Houyhnhnms, his disbelief in Newton's system and
> every sort of machine, Goldsmith and his delight in the particulars of
> common life that shocked his contemporaries, Burke with his con-
> viction that all states not grown slowly like a forest tree are tyrannies,
> found in England an opposite that stung their own thought into
> expression and made it lucid.[2]

In 1926 Yeats wrote a series of love poems, *A Man Young and Old*, the
'wild regrets for youth and love of an old man'. These poems are auto-
biographical, 'First Love'[3] and 'Human Dignity'[4] developing the image
of the stone (also used in connection with Maud Gonne in 'Easter,
1916') which appears in 'The Friends of his Youth'[5] and 'His Wildness'.[6]
The imagery of the poems is simple, and possibly influenced by residence
in Ballylee: old thorn-trees, old Madge coming down the lane, beds of
straw as well as down, the hare and pack, a bit of stone under a broken
tree. The result is a direct statement of 'what I dared not think / When
my blood was strong'. The simplicity creates vividness, it matches
memories of past emotional intensity with the brutal realism of age:

> The first of all the tribe lay there
> And did such pleasure take—
> She who had brought great Hector down

[1] *CP*, 267.   [2] W. B. Yeats, *Essays 1931–1936*, p. 36.
[3] *CP*, 249.   [4] *CP*, 250.   [5] *CP*, 252.   [6] *CP*, 254.

> And put all Troy to wreck—
> That she cried into this ear,
> 'Strike me if I shriek'.

The complementary series, *A Woman Young and Old*, places greater emphasis on the physical element of love in 'A Last Confession',[1] 'Consolation',[2] 'Parting',[3] though this emphasis is blended with ideas from *A Vision* in 'Before the World Was Made',[4] 'A First Confession',[5] 'Her Triumph'[6] and 'Chosen'.[7]

His 'Crazy Jane' poems contained in *Words for Music Perhaps*, came from a great burst of creative activity which began in the spring of 1929 and continued into the autumn of 1931. The views of love attributed to Crazy Jane (founded upon 'Cracked Mary', an old woman who lived in Gort, 'the local satirist and a really terrible one') are in part Yeats's own: she speaks from a fuller peasant physicality than the persona of *A Woman Young and Old*. Anti-clerical, anti-intellectual, she sees love as a conflict between opposites, yet also a reconciliation, a way to unity. The emphasis of these poems is upon desecration:

> 'Fair and foul are near of kin
> And fair needs foul,' I cried.[8]

Some of these poems owe a good deal to Blake's idea of contrariety, some to his imagery. 'Crazy Jane Talks with the Bishop' has shocked some readers with its 'place of excrement', but this comes from Blake (the line in *Jerusalem* 'For I will make their places of love and joy excrementitious') just as obviously as 'Girl's Song'[9] does, with its query 'Saw I an old man young / Or young man old?'

The vigorous affirmation of sexuality in these poems is accompanied by tenderness and a sense of blessedness, qualities that emerge in 'Lullaby',[10] a poem full of Yeats's inversions, his use of 'that', his repetitions, open and disguised, his stanza linkage and his cadences. The technical control of such a poem sweeps its reader along, its ease born of a confidence that has tamed rhetoric into conversational tones. 'After Long Silence'[11] and 'Mad as the Mist and Snow'[12] share this sense of stylised talk.

---

[1] *CP*, 313.   [2] *CP*, 310.   [3] *CP*, 311.   [4] *CP*, 308.
[5] *CP*, 309.   [6] *CP*, 310.   [7] *CP*, 311.
[8] 'Crazy Jane Talks with the Bishop', *CP*, 294.
[9] *CP*, 296.   [10] *CP*, 300.   [11] *CP*, 301.   [12] *CP*, 301.

11. *A Full Moon in March*

Another burst of activity in 1934 produced a series of metaphysical poems grouped as *Supernatural Songs*: obscure thought, brilliant lines and a Donne-like questioning. 'Whence had they come?'[1] depends upon the thought of *A Vision*, as does 'Meru'.[2] 'Ribh at the Tomb of Baile and Aillinn'[3] is a reworking of a Gaelic legend, of Swedenborg's description of the intercourse of angels (also suggested in 'Ribh Denounces Patrick'[4] and 'Ribh in Ecstasy'[5]), and of Yeats's own concern with the 'conflagration of the whole body'. These poems condense his ideas and gain their effect by directness and strength. 'The Four Ages of Man', for instance, is a superb poem, classic in simplicity:

> He with body waged a fight,
> But body won; it walks upright.
>
> Then he struggled with the heart;
> Innocence and peace depart.
>
> Then he struggled with the mind;
> His proud heart he left behind.
>
> Now his wars on God begin;
> At stroke of midnight God shall win.[6]

The four stanzas, however, represent, in Yeats's thinking, the four questions of *A Vision*'s twenty-eight phases of the Moon, Earth, Water, Air and Fire, and these in turn represent four types of civilisation: an early nature-dominated civilisation; a chivalric period; the Renaissance to the nineteenth-century period; and the 'purging away of our civilisation by our hatred'.

12. *Last Poems*

After 1929 Yeats no longer used the Tower as a summer residence. With Lady Gregory's death his connection with the west of Ireland diminished; her death left a vacuum in his life, and he missed the quiet of Coole. In 1933 he bought a small house and grounds, Riversdale, at the foot of the Dublin mountains, and began to live out still more

---

[1] *CP*, 332.   [2] *CP*, 333.   [3] *CP*, 327.
[4] *CP*, 328.   [5] *CP*, 329.   [6] *CP*, 332.

dreams of his youth and some of his middle age.[1] 'What Then?' conveys something of his delight in this place:

> All his happier dreams came true—
> A small old house, wife, daughter, son,
> Grounds where plum and cabbage grew,
> Poets and wits about him drew;
> 'What then?' sang Plato's ghost 'What then?'[2]

And one of the remarkable answers to thinking of death was the prayer of 'An Acre of Grass':

> Grant me an old man's frenzy,
> Myself must I remake
> Till I am Timon and Lear
> Or that William Blake
> Who beat upon the wall
> Till Truth obeyed his call.[3]

Illness kept breaking in on Yeats's last years: heart, blood pressure, nephritis, congestion of the lungs. He spent winters abroad in search of health. Behind his poetry another forward-looking thought of middle age was working; could he, knowing how frail his vigour had been from youth, copy Landor's old age? It is out of a resulting determination to be active that he writes 'The Spur',[4] with its confession that 'lust and rage' motivate his poetry, an idea reinforced by poems like 'The Wild Old Wicked Man'[5] and put some years earlier, in 'A Prayer for Old Age'[6] with its wish that he might seem though he died old 'a foolish passionate man'.

Rage possessed him in the poems upon the Casement Diaries; he took up this mask with passion, and with irony when he returned to Parnell in 'Come Gather Round Me, Parnellites'[7] and the brief epigrammatic 'Parnell'.[8] These poems are unlike 'Parnell's Funeral',[9] a magnificent piece of work (written between 1932 and 1933) which blends an old dream,[10] an old poem of his which echoed a saying of Goethe's ('To a Shade'),[11] and material from Frazer's *Golden Bough* about heart eating,

[1] W. B. Yeats, *Essays*, p. 506.   [2] *CP*, 347.   [3] *CP*, 346.

[4] *CP*, 359.   [5] *CP*, 356.   [6] *CP*, 326.   [7] *CP*, 355.

[8] *CP*, 359.   [9] *CP*, 319.

[10] W. B. Yeats, *Autobiographies* 1926, p. 458.   [11] *CP*, 123.

and links the whole to Ireland, caught in the remorseless gyres of historical change, her leaders now destroyed not by strangers but by their own people because 'An age is the reversal of an age'. The poem itself is enriched by the bitter wisdom Yeats had learned, like Swift, from contemplation of Irish politics.

The idea of the overthrow of civilization kept pressing in on Yeats. The earlier plangency of his cry that 'Man is in love and loves what vanishes' gives way to a deliberate carelessness in 'The Gyres', an assumption of not caring:

> Conduct and work grow coarse, and coarse the soul,
> What matter . . .[1]

The command from the sage in the cavern is 'Rejoice' and the laughter that greets the fall of Troy, the loss of gracious civilisation at any time, and particularly the present, is tragic joy. There is some balance to be found in the idea of continuity as it occurs in 'Lapis Lazuli':

> All things fall and are built again,
> And those that build them again are gay.[2]

In general, however, despite the apparent detachment, unease, sorrow, anger, lurk behind the façade: they break through in 'The Curse of Cromwell',[3] in the disappointments of 'Why should not old men be mad?',[4] in the contemplation of the bust of Maud Gonne by Oliver Sheppard in 'A Bronze Head'.[5] 'Are you content?'[6] answers the problem as simply as Goldsmith did by saying before his death that his mind was not at ease, for in this poem Yeats sums up his work before the judgment of his ancestors and ends 'But I am not content'.

Discontent emerges too in 'The Circus Animals' Desertion',[7] where Yeats looks back on his early themes from the Gaelic legends, 'that sea-rider Oisin led by the nose' written by a boy in love with the idea of love, then *The Countess Cathleen*, written by Maud Gonne's hopeless adorer, his dreams perhaps broken by the Fool and Blind Man whom Maud had favoured, the solution for life emerging through work at the theatre. The analysis of how all this had come about is devastating; the images may have grown 'in pure mind' but arose out of 'the foul rag-and-bone shop of the heart'.

Yeats, however, ran his course between opposites, and his praise of life is at its best when he remembers his friends. 'Beautiful Lofty Things' is

[1] *CP*, 337.   [2] *CP*, 338.   [3] *CP*, 350.   [4] *CP*, 388.
[5] *CP*, 382.   [6] *CP*, 370.   [7] *CP*, 391.

an example of his economy; here he draws his friends larger than life and contrives to invest them with uniqueness, dramatising a single moment of memory and investing it with symbolic meaning. This is his old technique at work, but even more directly than before. The distinction between literary symbol and personal experience has been eliminated.

> . . . Maud Gonne at Howth station waiting a train,
> Pallas Athene in that straight back and arrogant head
> All the Olympians; a thing never known again.[1]

The past literary symbol is almost no longer needed, because his images, the images of his own life, are enough. They fill the canvas of 'The Municipal Gallery Revisited' and they can convey to us the emotions he felt at seeing the portraits of his friends largely because his own thoughts and memories are allowed to comment upon his relationships with them:

> You that would judge me, do not judge alone
> This book or that, come to this hallowed place
> Where my friends' portraits hang and look thereon;
> Ireland's history in their lineaments trace;
> Think where man's glory most begins and ends,
> And say my glory was I had such friends.[2]

In the midst of writing poems such as 'In Tara's Halls',[3] which read as though they were exercises for facing imminent death, Yeats enjoyed himself with vigorous eight-line stanzas in 'Three Songs to the One Burden',[4] which recapture the early vigour of the Crazy Jane period. Other poems which have this singing air to them are 'The Pilgrim',[5] 'Colonel Martin'[6] and 'The O'Rahilly',[7] where the refrain is effective. In contrast to these is 'The Statues',[8] an example of Yeats's best sort of historical poem, his imagination ranging freely and seizing upon details which give an immediate impact to his often involved thoughts. In 'The Statues' he is tracing the effect of artistic principle upon action, referring Ireland to the example of Greece, and giving his theme its excitement through the skilful use of visual imagery:

> the banks of oars that swam upon
> The many-headed foam at Salamis.

[1] CP, 348.   [2] CP, 368.   [3] CP, 374.   [4] CP, 371.
[5] CP, 360.   [6] CP, 361.   [7] CP, 354.   [8] CP, 375.

This pictorial quality emerges in 'News for the Delphic Oracle',[1] a reworking of 'The Delphic Oracle on Plotinus'[2] with a blend of Yeats's personal usage of Gaelic mythology, and the Poussin picture of the marriage of Peleus and Thetis. But Yeats's ability to move in and out of history, to refer it above all to Ireland, is supremely at work in 'Under Ben Bulben'.[3]

This poem is an amalgam of most of Yeats's interests. The sages apostrophised in the opening stanza are probably a mixture of the Christian hermits, the monks of the Thebaid (mentioned earlier in 'Demon and Beast',[4] a poem which virtually echoes the Christian command to render unto Caesar the things that are Caesar's), of whom Yeats read in books by J. O. Hannay. The word Mareotic is a link between this idea and Shelley's *The Witch of Atlas*, one of Yeats's favourite early poems; the witch symbolised the beauty of wisdom. The horsemen and women probably come out of memories of the stories of Mary Battle, an old housekeeper who saw visionary beings; in the poem they ride the dawn 'Where Ben Bulben sets the scene'. This is a cue to return to the theme in Irish terms, the theme of the universal memory, the idea of Anima Mundi to which Yeats's mind always holds strongly, into which both peace and war return the dead. It is a consolatory almost defiantly held belief, and it leads to the third stanza, which makes use of Ireland's violence to create an image of momentary ease. The fourth stanza returns to the idea of 'The Statues' and to Yeats's insistence upon the significance of the dream, and to the artist's part in its working out, a working out which is subject to the gyres of history.

The fifth stanza reverts to the 'ancient Ireland' of the second stanza, giving Yeats's own attitude to its history, with its stern advice to Irish poets to learn their trade (an echo perhaps of 'What then?' which describes his twenties as 'crammed with toil'). Their song is to be of the peasanty and gentry, the rogues and monks, the lords and ladies of Anglo-Irish Ireland: all this will maintain the indomitable quality of the seven heroic centuries (since the Normans came to Ireland in 1167) against what may befall.

The poem sums up much that Yeats had thought and written; it reminds us of his comment that he had spent his life saying the same thing in different ways. The final part of the poem returns to Ben Bulben and Yeats's grave in Drumcliff Churchyard, to the Sligo area, a place of great changing natural beauty where legend lived on the lips of storytellers or

[1] *CP*, 376.   [2] *CP*, 306.   [3] *CP*, 397.   [4] *CP*, 209.

in the lives of individuals, where Yeats had formed his youth, dreamed and believed—or wanted to believe—in the supernatural. The three final lines imply that a cold eye is to be cast on life and on death because this is the ultimate challenge which he had been facing all his life and which he thought must be faced with bravery, with heroic indifference, with the aristocratic disdain of the horseman.

This is the attitude of 'The Gyres'[1] and of 'The Apparitions'[2] also, but 'The Man and the Echo'[3] is perhaps the greatest, certainly the most hauntingly moving, of all Yeats's poems on death. It, too, is set in Sligo. The cleft that's christened Alt is on Ben Bulben; its echoes in the mind are those of Delphi, and the poet has reached the stage of asking himself questions about his life and failing to answer them. The *Echo* sounds twice; its whisper is that of death and of 'the increasing·Night / That opens her mystery and her fright'.[4] The first echo with its note of death is answered with that indomitable intellectual energy which works upon itself until it knows all work is done. And then there is the great human cry in the face of the night: not now the bravado of 'What matter?' but the '*What then?*' of Plato's ghost. Yeats could not become a Christian, he could not 'choose for his belief / What seems most welcome in the tomb'; and his heterodox pursuit of wisdom withered into his own truth, into what was for him the Homeric honesty of knowing merely that he did not know:

> All that I have said and done,
> Now that I am old and ill,
> Turns into a question till
> I lie awake night after night
> And never get the answers right.
> Did that play of mine send out
> Certain men the English shot?
> Did words of mine put too great strain
> On that woman's reeling brain?
> Could my spoken words have checked
> That whereby a house lay wrecked?
> And all seems evil until I
> Sleepless would lie down and die.
> Lie down and die.

[1] *CP*, 337. [2] *CP*, 386.
[3] *CP*, 393. [4] 'The Apparitions', *CP*, 386.

Echo

Lie down and die.

Man

> That were to shirk
> The spiritual intellect's great work,
> And shirk it in vain. There is no release
> In a bodkin or disease,
> Nor can there be work so great
> As that which cleans man's dirty slate.
> While man can still his body keep
> Wine or love drug him to sleep,
> Waking he thanks the Lord that he
> Has body and its stupidity,
> But body gone he sleeps no more,
> And till his intellect grows sure
> That all's arranged in one clear view,
> Pursues the thoughts that I pursue,
> Then stands in judgment on his soul,
> And, all work done, dismisses all
> Out of intellect and sight
> And sinks at last into the night.

Echo

Into the night.

Man

> O Rocky Voice,
> Shall we in that great night rejoice?
> What do we know but that we face
> One another in this place?
> But hush, for I have lost the theme,
> Its joy or night seem but a dream;
> Up there some hawk or owl has struck,
> Dropping out of sky or rock,
> A stricken rabbit is crying out,
> And its cry distracts my thought.

Select Bibliography

Those poems of W. B. Yeats not included in *Collected Poems*, 1950, or *Selected Poems* (ed. Jeffares), 1961, or *Selected Poetry* (ed. Jeffares), 1962, can be read in P. Allt and R. K. Alspach, *The Variorum Edition of the Poems of W. B. Yeats*, 1957. This is indispensable for readers who want to compare the many different published versions of poems which Yeats rewrote from time to time.

Further information about the poems and other writings can be found in Allan Wade, *A Bibliography of the Writings of W. B. Yeats*, 1951, and *The Letters of W. B. Yeats*, ed. Allan Wade, 1954, also give useful information about particular poems.

Critical Works

Bradford, Curtis. *Yeats at Work*, 1965

Ellmann, Richard. *Yeats: The Man and the Masks*, 1949

Ellmann, Richard. *The Identity of Yeats*, 1954

Henn, T. R. *The Lonely Tower: Studies in the Poetry of W. B. Yeats*, 1950

Hone, J. M. *W. B. Yeats 1865–1939*, 1942

Jeffares, A. Norman. *W. B. Yeats: Man and Poet*, 1949; revised edition, 1963

   A Commentary on the Collected Poems of W. B. Yeats, 1968

Jeffares, A. Norman and Knowland, A. S. *A Commentary on the Plays of W. B. Yeats*, 1975

Kermode, Frank. *Romantic Image*, 1957

Melchiori, Giorgio. *The Whole Mystery of Art: Pattern into Poetry in the Works of W. B. Yeats*, 1960

Stallworthy, J. *Between the Lines*, 1963

Stock, A. G. *W. B. Yeats: his poetry and thought*, 1961

Torchiana, Donald T. *Yeats and Georgian Ireland*, 1966

Ure, Peter. *Towards a Mythology: Studies in the Poetry of W. B. Yeats*, 1946

Wilson, F. A. C. *W. B. Yeats and Tradition*, 1958

Wilson, F. A. C. *Yeats's Iconography*, 1960